USA Stars & Lights
Portraits from the Dark

A LIGHTHOUSE PHOTOGRAPHY COLLECTION

DAVID ZAPATKA

A United States Lighthouse Society Publication
Graphic Design by Richard Gales

United States Lighthouse Society
Hansville, Washington

Printed in the United States of America
Back cover photo of David Zapatka courtesy Dante Bellini, Jr.
USA Stars & Lights: Portraits from the Dark
Copyright © 2020 David Zapatka
All rights reserved. No production of this book may be reproduced, stored in a retrieval system, or transmitted in any form by any means electronic, mechanical, photocopy, recording, or other except for brief quotations in printed previews, without prior permission of the publisher.

ISBN: 978-0-578-76297-5

Table of Contents

Foreword . . . . Page 1

Introduction . . . . Page 3

Dedication . . . . Page 7

Memorial - Robert Izzo . . . . Page 8

Portraits from the Dark Gallery . . . Page 9

Lighthouse Adventures . . . . Page 95

Acknowledgments . . . . Page 144

Index . . . . Page 148

FOREWORD

Light.

In its many forms, light pervades and shapes our lives. It reveals, it guides, it explores, it uplifts – it illuminates our path in so many ways.

Its antithesis, darkness – the absence of light, not a thing in itself – can bring peace, quiet and rest, but it also can bring danger. That's especially true for a mariner approaching a coastline, and it's the reason America encircled itself with a necklace of lights for the safety of life at sea.

David Zapatka, in this and his earlier book *Stars & Lights: Darkest of Dark Nights*, explores the intersection of darkness and light that defines that necklace. His journey through his Stars and Lights Project has been long and sometimes difficult, but the images he has captured show the lighthouses of America as they were meant to be seen – as beacons shining against the backdrop of the night, often against stunning starry skies that remind us that the universe, too, needs its beacons of light amid the darkness.

Lighthouses are daymarks too, of course, and almost all photographs, tourist and professional alike, capture them in their daytime shapes and colors. It takes technical skill to properly image lighthouses at work, as they were meant to be seen. David brings that skill, honed by experience, to this collection of nighttime photographs from light stations he has sought out – dare I say it – in their darkest hours.

American philosopher Loren Eiseley once wrote that "if there is magic on this planet, it is contained in water." That's true, but that magic, I believe, is most concentrated at the edges of things, at the place where water meets land. Lighthouses mark that boundary, that edge. And they bring their own magic, one born not only of the intersection of land and water, but of darkness and light.

If there is magic in this universe, it is contained in light.

Lighthouses have brought that light to America's coasts since colonial times. Many of them are fading now, as the technology of light and of energy beyond the limits of visible light changes the ways things are imaged. Radar and satellite navigation guide large ships, and many smaller ones, these days. For a long time, many lighthouses simply were replaced with newer and simpler automated beacons or decommissioned entirely, and left untended. Often, they deteriorated. But untended doesn't always mean uncared for, and in the early 1980s a lighthouse preservation movement began to grow.

There is a new generation of lightkeepers now. They are preservationists, part of a wider movement that recognizes the value of the visible reminders of our past, the markers on our national and cultural journey through time. Old techniques and methods have been revived to apply repairs authentic to the aging towers across the land, and a handful of accomplished lampists remains to pass along the secrets of the now-outmoded but still stunningly beautiful Fresnel lenses that once guarded our coasts, and sometimes still do.

I'm one of those lightkeepers. I am not only honored to lead the United States Lighthouse Society, I tend two lighthouses in Buffalo Harbor. The Buffalo Lighthouse Association installed a new lens and relit the city's iconic 1833 lighthouse just a few years ago, as that urban waterfront enjoys its own renaissance. It is now not just a light from the past, but a beacon for the future. That's perhaps a new role for lighthouses – but one that fits very well with the ancient lighthouse role of marking places of coming and going, of journeys outward bound toward change and journeys back to the familiar touchstones of safe harbor and home.

As a lightkeeper, I appreciate David's photographic journeys as well. If we preserve these icons, so does he – in beautiful images that capture why we all do what we do, and why we make the sacrifices most of us make as volunteers to keep these lights burning. The light they send into the darkness speaks of our rich national maritime heritage, and of the futures we navigate as individuals and as a nation. David captures that light, and paints it against the deeper perspective of night skies studded with the timeless light of the stars. Looking at these images can be truly humbling. And if it motivates you to visit a lighthouse, or contribute to its support, so much the better.

David is a lightkeeper, too. Just look through these pages, for his photographs that not only capture a moment of light, but capture the meaning of the lights as well. David works magic with the lens on his camera – but it's the lens of understanding that he brings to his quest that really makes him a lightkeeper. Share that understanding. Enjoy the beauty – but recognize, as well, that what these images portray is your heritage too. In its earliest years America was built at the boundary of land and water – and it grew by defining that boundary by bringing light to the darkness.

And that legacy still shines.

Michael N. Vogel President, United States Lighthouse Society

Introduction

This captivating experience has everything to do with sights and sounds occurring deep into the night. Standing in front of you, a historic tower with its bright light flashing every few seconds, simultaneously sending its magnified beam twenty miles out to sea. You realize the waves crashing onto the rocks forty feet below. Then a breeze coming off the water caresses your face as the salty ocean aroma ignites your sense of smell. Soon you hear a boat motoring off in the distance. Nearby, the American flag luffs in the breeze as your camera fires away. Click. Click. Click. Above all that has touched you hangs a majestic sky filled with millions of stars as far as your eyes can see. Time seems indifferent as the enormity of the universe lies before you. Suddenly, you feel really small, practically insignificant.

When this adventure began in 2013, I had no big plan, but rather a simple, personal artistic challenge to determine the possibility of capturing a local lighthouse at night, accented by whatever stars chose to appear above. The genre of nighttime imagery was gaining ground throughout the photographic world, and the initial shoots enlightened my understanding of all the camera could achieve. That year began something I never imagined and has now covered thousands of miles to bring me to this next journey. Four years later, in 2017, we published the first book, *Stars & Lights: Darkest of Dark Nights*, in which we showcased 130 landscape night lighthouse images. Here, we've expanded on that piece by presenting all of the photographs in portrait orientation. While some may look familiar to the first book, for the most part, these images are previously unpublished.

Initially, photographing Rhode Island's lighthouses was relatively easy, as it's the smallest state geographically. When we explored beyond the state and into those in the entire Northeast, we soon realized that it is a lighthouse-dense area boasting close to 150 lighthouses within two to three hours of Rhode Island's borders. As a result, we found ourselves taking longer trips and adding to the collection. Our excitement building, we arranged to broaden the scope to a national level, reaching lighthouses in seventeen states. Unfortunately, in March 2020, Covid-19 hit the US, halting our travels. Ironically, I achieved most of the first photographs in complete solitude, deep into the night, on the grounds of each lighthouse...socially distanced from others.

Castle Hill Lighthouse, Newport, RI with NEOWISE Comet, July 2020

Over time, though, I realized some shoots held potential physical danger, which led me to partner with other photographers. Yet, in a Covid world, travel, which includes hotels, restaurants, rest stops, as well as meetings with people such as lighthouse foundation directors or keepers, posed health threats not worth taking.

Tchefuncte River, Madisonville, Louisiana

The first seven years of Stars & Lights, long before any pandemic restrictions, had a natural flow, traveling between subjects with ease. Along the way, many wonderful people came into my life, including those associated with the United States Lighthouse Society. Within that network, I met Mike Vogel, then the head of the Buffalo Main Lighthouse and now the current Society president, while traveling through western New York State, hoping to photograph this new addition to my list. Though I may have appeared a bit crazy, he assisted me in numerous ways, including inviting me to the Society's National Convention in New Orleans to present my project to its members. Immediately, I began to research lighthouses in that area which lead to photographing four, including the Tchefuncte River lighthouse. Its location is accessed only by boat, creating some logistical problems for me, especially arriving from across the country. With some kismet on my side and a week before the conference, I received a call from area resident, Dall Thomas. Dall wanted to purchase my first book directly through me. During our conversation, I asked where he lived, and when he said New Orleans, I queried if he had a boat. He did! On an unusually clear New Orleans evening, Dall met me at a boat ramp with his small Boston Whaler, and together we shuttled a short distance to the lighthouse. It was a beautiful Lake Pontchartrain night with my shooting the lighthouse while Dall lit the scene under my direction. I then shared my rare image of the Tchefuncte River Lighthouse with the Society during my presentation the next morning. The lighthouse director approached me after the talk to express her gratitude, saying no one had ever before photographed there at night. Time and again, such situations have occurred as many lighthouses are, as they say, off the beaten path. Two years later, I relish this moment, and still enjoy saying "Tchefuncte!"

Travel throughout the country is nothing new for me. For more than forty years, I've been a television cameraman for news and sports programs, first, for a decade at the local level, then in 1990, I made the jump to the networks. Camera work is pretty much anonymous unless the show runs credits, and it's likely you've unknowingly seen some of my work throughout the years on ABC, NBC, CBS, HBO, CNN, and PBS. For twenty straight years, I worked the Men's NCAA Final Four National Basketball Championship on CBS, and each spring would travel the country shooting all things basketball. The camera work has brought me to more than 30 countries, and to every state but West Virginia. I recently learned a lighthouse was erected there a few years ago, giving me a good reason to finally visit. Maybe it'll be in the next book.

Long before making the leap into television, as a fifth grader, I purchased a 35mm camera on a whim. The yearbook advisor saw the camera around my neck and asked me to shoot for their staff. I then received my first press credential, a permanent hall pass, along with free film and processing. I was hooked. Still photography instantly became a significant part of my life, and remains so to this day.

Nearly three decades later in 2001, I joined a small group dedicated to preserving a century-old lighthouse on Rhode Island's Narragansett Bay. At one point, this lighthouse, the Plum Beach Lighthouse, was on the Lighthouse Digest Doomsday List of historic properties at high risk for destruction due to neglect and decay. A generous State grant afforded its renovation in 2003, and the spearheading group, the Friends of Plum Beach Lighthouse, elected me its president in 2004. We even created a character we called "Plummy", a seven-foot tall mascot to broaden awareness of our fundraising efforts. Plummy often receives invitations to parades and events, and is wildly popular with the younger children. Then in 2010, our group petitioned the State's General Assembly to start a Lighthouse License Plate Program which successfully raised more than quarter million dollars to date to preserve Plum Beach Lighthouse.

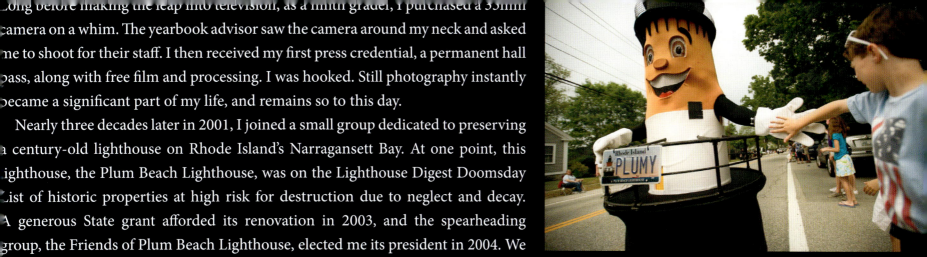

Plum Beach Lighthouse mascot, Plummy, marching in a parade.

Alone on Narragansett Bay and under the cover of darkness during a new moon night in 2013, I ventured by boat to Dutch Island, considered part of Jamestown, Rhode Island, about a mile south of Plum Beach Lighthouse. Here, I photographed the island lighthouse under the brilliance of the Milky Way. I shared my images with a local Coast Guard station chief I met through the lighthouse work. Together we marveled what the camera captured. That moment marked the start of the lighthouse journey…one with no end in sight. With more than 800 lighthouses sprawled throughout America, this project will continue to enthrall me. Eventually the entire lighthouse collection will be housed in the United States Lighthouse Society Candace Clifford Memorial Digital Archives, and will be publicly available for all.

Dutch Island, Jamestown, RI

Within these pages are 169-night lighthouse images, some of which are both unique and rare. The unique ones, among which are Race Rock, Esopus Meadows, Long Island, and Stratford Shoal, are a few of the many presented here that have never been captured on film at night. The rare ones required the right tools for the job: access to a boat, a special 20-foot water-based tripod, and a willingness by me and my small team to take extraordinary measures to properly light each one while on location using a single exposure. There is no Photoshop used in the production of these images. I took more than seven years to successfully capture these lighthouses in an accomplishment shared by many who helped along the way.

Though I claim this publication presents 169 lighthouses, in truth, aficionados could argue the count is really 166. The Kennebec River Range Light has two towers on the property and is one of the few operating pairs left in the country. More people recognize the front tower and overlook the rear light displayed in photographs. Here, each tower has its own image, causing one "lighthouse" to be represented as two. Then on Thacher Island, off Rockport, Massachusetts, twin lighthouses, both still lighted, stand. For this book, I separate these into three images. While they should be presented together in a photograph, each tower is also distinct in its own right. Hence, the Thacher Island lighthouses are presented as the twins, the north tower, and the south tower.

Regarding the book's layout, I encourage people to look at the collection in its entirety as more of an important historical essay. A number of the lighthouses are popular tourist spots. However, I consider them lonely sentinels of the night that continue their posts in the manner for which most were built. Unfortunately, the government's divesting of these beauties requires private citizens to protect our endangered monuments. I laid out the images to create a comfortable flow from one to the next, capturing the lighthouses that still shine as lighted beacons, such as all of those in Massachusetts. However, lighthouses no longer lit, known as "standing lighthouses" are not represented here. They simply lack the dynamic nature of the lighted ones. Following the image gallery, I include narratives of how each photograph was captured, both technically and aesthetically. At times, elements of danger or loneliness existed, but every time, the striking beauty of the lighthouses made each one worthwhile. If you pick up this book, say in a doctor's office while waiting for an appointment, scanning the images will bring visual pleasure. Should you be further intrigued, it may be worthwhile to read about each lighthouse adventure found at the back of the book.

These monuments exemplify not only beauty, but throughout history, have come to symbolize hope, a way forward from any adversity, whether on sea or land. Creating this collection has been my calling over the last seven years, and presenting them to you is an honor. My hope is to continue for many years to come.

The NEOWISE Comet and Dutch Island Lighthouse, Jamestown, Rhode Island, June 2020

For Chloe and Juliet
May you always dream big,
and may all those dreams come true.

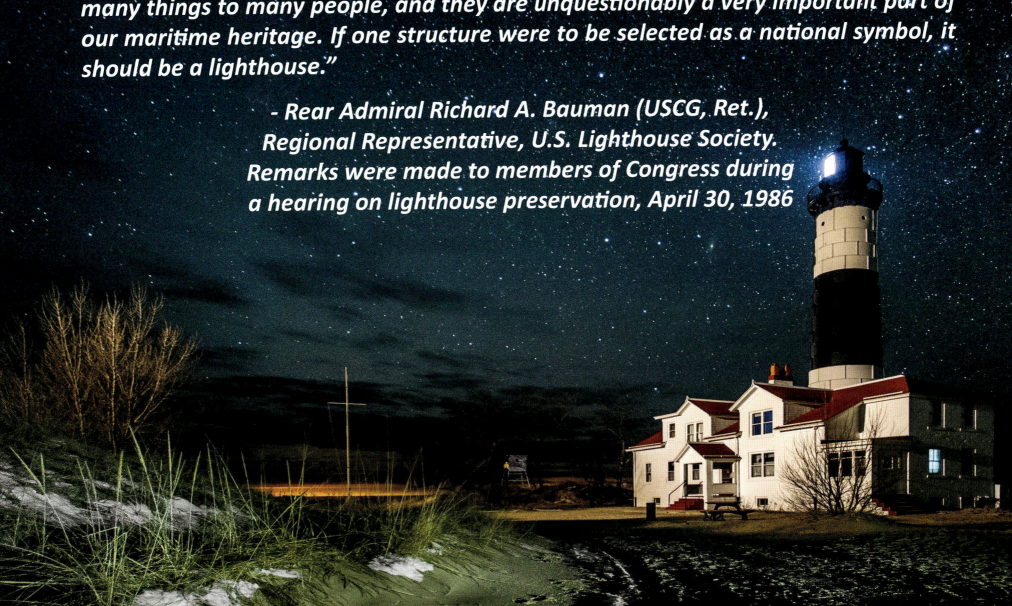

USA Stars & Lights Gallery

"We feel that lighthouses are one of the most unique structures ever constructed by man. They transcend all classes of people and all national borders. Lighthouses are many things to many people, and they are unquestionably a very important part of our maritime heritage. If one structure were to be selected as a national symbol, it should be a lighthouse."

- Rear Admiral Richard A. Bauman (USCG, Ret.),
Regional Representative, U.S. Lighthouse Society.
Remarks were made to members of Congress during
a hearing on lighthouse preservation, April 30, 1986

Race Point, Provincetown, Massachusetts

North Light, Block Island, Rhode Island

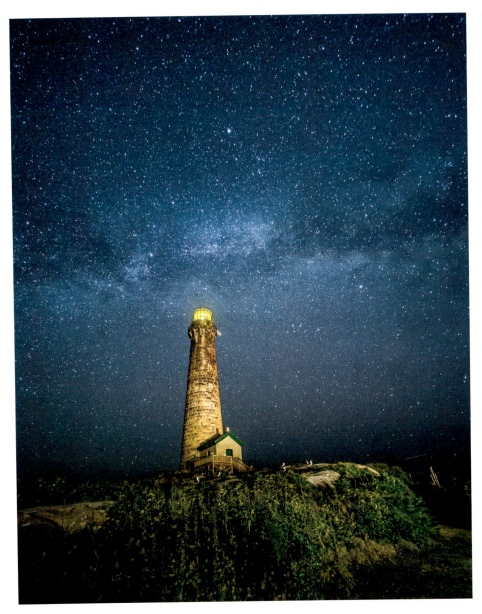

Thacher Island North, Rockport, Massachusetts

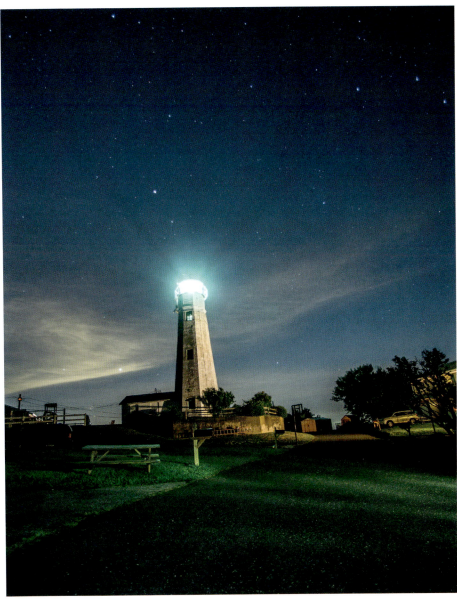

Eatons Neck, Northport, New York

Windmill Point, Alburgh, Vermont

Sleepy Hollow, Tarrytown, New York

Squirrel Point, Arrowsic, Maine

Sandy Hook, Highlands, New Jersey

Cove Point, Lusby, Maryland

Cape Elizabeth, Maine

Barnegat, Long Beach, New Jersey

Fort Gratiot, Port Huron, Michigan

Sandy Neck, Barnstable, Massachusetts

East Point, Maurice River Township, New Jersey

Biloxi, Mississippi

Huntington Harbor, Huntington, New York

Point Judith, Narragansett, Rhode Island

Southwest Ledge, New Haven, Connecticut

Piney Point, Maryland *Avery Point, Groton, Connecticut*

Horton Point, Southold, New York

Castle Hill, Newport, Rhode Island

Long Point, Provincetown, Massachusetts

Wood End, Provincetown, Massachusetts

Tongue Point, Bridgeport, Connecticut

Edgartown Harbor, Martha's Vineyard, Massachusetts

Cleveland Ledge, West Falmouth, Massachusetts

Absecon, Atlantic City, New Jersey

Stratford Shoal, Long Island Sound, Connecticut

Nauset, Eastham, Massachusetts

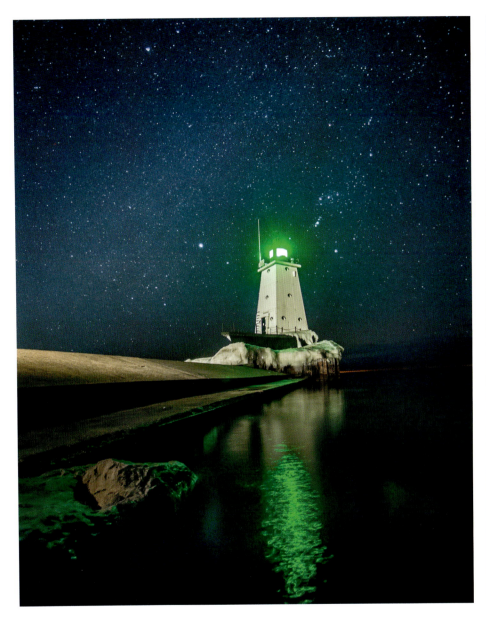

Ludington North Breakwater, Ludington, Michigan

Sodus Bay, Sodus Point, New York

Old Saybrook Breakwater, Old Saybrook, Connecticut

Thacher Island South, Rockport, Massachusetts

Portsmouth Harbor, Portsmouth, New Hampshire

Nubble, Cape Neddick, York, Maine

Lynde Point, Old Saybrook, Connecticut

Ten Pound Island, Gloucester, Massachusetts

Fenwick Island, Delaware *Bluff Point, Vancour Island, New York*

Stepping Stones, Kings Point, New York

Borden Flats, Fall River, Massachusetts

Sandy Point, Prudence Island, Rhode Island

North Pier, Erie, Pennsylvania

Romer Shoal, Ambrose Channel, New Jersey

Sakonnet, Little Compton, Rhode Island

Livingstone Memorial, Detroit, Michigan   *Turtle Rock, Philadelphia, Pennsylvania*

Rondout Creek, Kingston, New York

Bird Island, Marion, Massachusetts

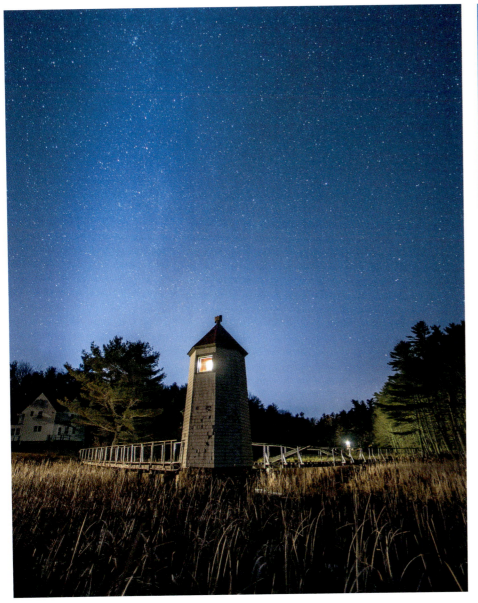
Kennebec River Front Range, Arrowsic, Maine

Kennebec River Rear Range, Arrowsic, Maine

Turkey Point, North East, Maryland

Brant Point, Nantucket, Massachusetts

New London Harbor, New London, Connecticut

Buffalo Main, Buffalo, New York

Plum Beach, North Kingstown, Rhode Island

Isle la Motte, Vermont

Palmer Island, New Bedford, Massachusetts

Greens Ledge, Norwalk, Connecticut

Big Sable, Ludington, Michigan

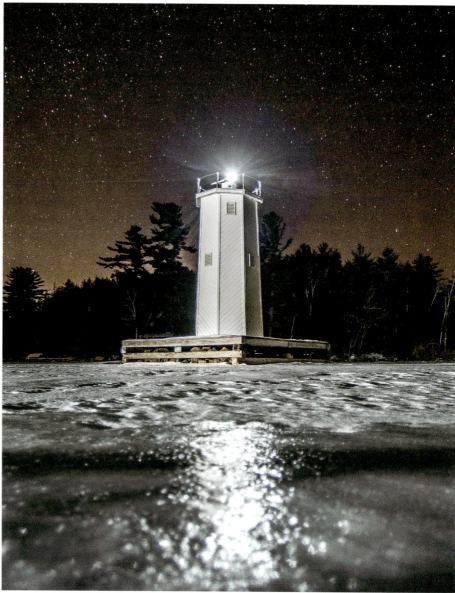

Burkehaven, Lake Sunapee, New Hampshire

Rose Island, Newport, Rhode Island

Drum Point, Solomon, Maryland

Boston, Massachusetts

Coney Island, Brooklyn, New York

Doubling Point, Arrowsic, Maine

Plymouth Bug, Plymouth, Massachusetts

West Quoddy, Lubec, Maine

Bakers Island, Salem, Massachusetts

Pomham Rocks, East Providence, Rhode Island

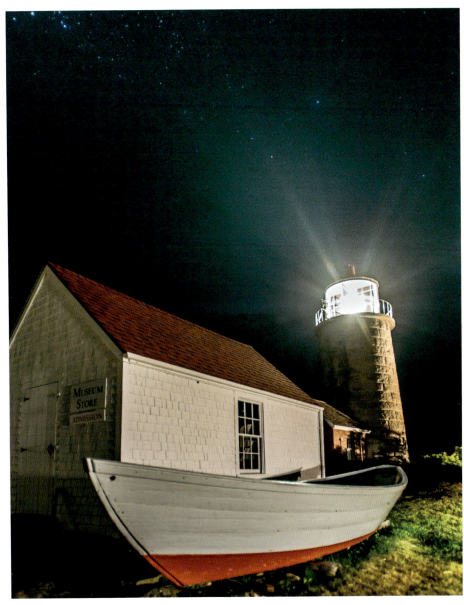

Monhegan Island, Maine

Hereford Inlet, Wildwood, New Jersey

Derby St. Wharf, Salem, Massachusetts

Little Sable, Mears, Michigan

New Canal, New Orleans, Louisiana

Saugerties, New York

Sea Girt, New Jersey

48

Scituate Harbor, Scituate, Massachusetts

Old Field Village, New York

Cape Poge, Chappaquiddick, Martha's Vineyard, Massachusetts

30 Mile Point, Barker, New York

Anniquam, Gloucester, Massachusetts

Port Sanilac, Michigan

Tarpaulin Cove, Gosnold, Massachusetts

Warwick Neck, Warwick, Rhode Island

Hog Island, Portsmouth, Rhode Island *Long Beach Bar, Southold, New York*

Hospital Point, Beverly, Massachusetts

Grosse Point, Evanston, Illinois

Little Gull, Southold, New York *Loon Island, Sunapee, New Hampshire*

Dunkirk, New York

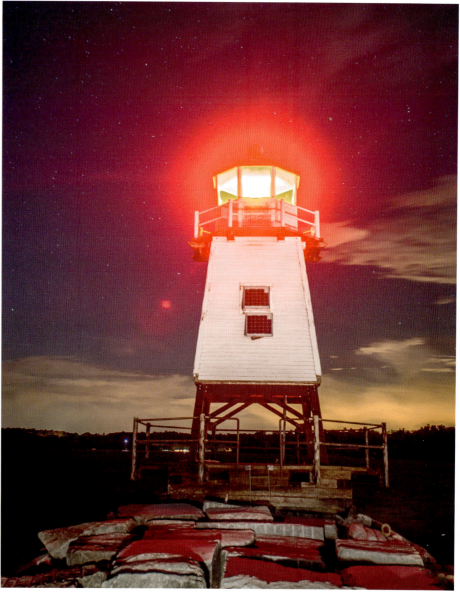

Burlington Harbor North, Burlington, Vermont

Charlotte Genesee, Rochester, New York

Peck Ledge, Norwalk, Connecticut

Marblehead, Massachusetts

Salmon River, Pulaski, New York

Montauk, New York

Nobska Point, Falmouth, Massachusetts

Gurnet, Plymouth, Massachusetts

White River, Whitehall, Michigan

Conimicut Point, Warwick, Rhode Island

Portland Bug, South Portland, Maine

Pemaquid Point, Bristol, Maine

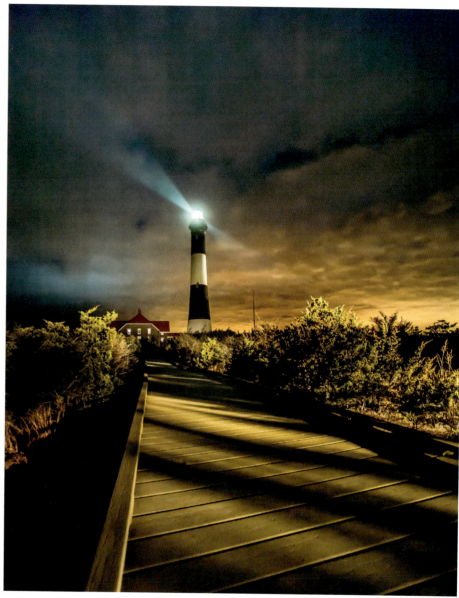

Fire Island, New York

Stratford Point, Stratford, Connecticut

Latimer Reef, Southold, New York

63

Plum Island, Newburyport, Massachusetts

Great Captain Island, Greenwich, Connecticut

Esopus Meadows, Port Ewen, New York

Presque Isle, Erie, Pennsylvania

Eastern Point, Gloucester, Massachusetts

Bass River, West Dennis, Massachusetts

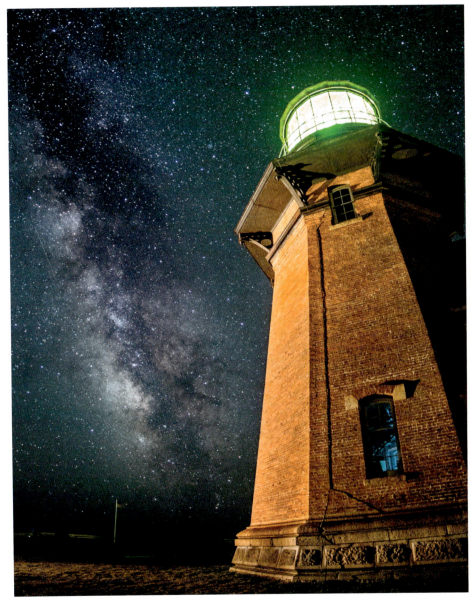

Southeast, Block Island, Rhode Island

Tinicum Rear Range, Paulsboro, New Jersey

Big Bay Point, Michigan

Kenosha North Pier, Kenosha, Wisconsin

West Chop, Martha's Vineyard, Massachusetts

Cumberland Head, Plattsburgh, New York

Navesink, Highlands, New Jersey

Aquinnah, Martha's Vineyard, Massachusetts

Cape May, New Jersey

Great Point, Nantucket, Massachusetts

Thacher Island Twins, Rockport, Massachusetts

Barcelona, Westfield, New York

Goat Island, Newport, Rhode Island *Orient Point, Orient, New York*

Herrick Cove, Lake Sunapee, New Hampshire

Ned's Point, Mattapoisett, Massachusetts

Owl's Head, Rockland, Maine

Gloucester Breakwater, Gloucester, Massachusetts

Dice Head, Castine, Maine

Hudson-Athens, Hudson, New York

New London Ledge, New London, Connecticut

Faulkner Island, Guilford, Connecticut

Straitsmouth Island, Rockport, Massachusetts

Tibbetts Point, Cape Vincent, New York

Highland, Truro, Massachusetts

Chatham, Massachusetts

North Dumpling Island, Southold, New York

Point Aux Barques, Port Hope, Michigan

Graves, Boston, Massachusetts

Verona Beach, New York

Sodus Point Museum, Sodus Point, New York

Fort Point, Stockton Springs, Maine

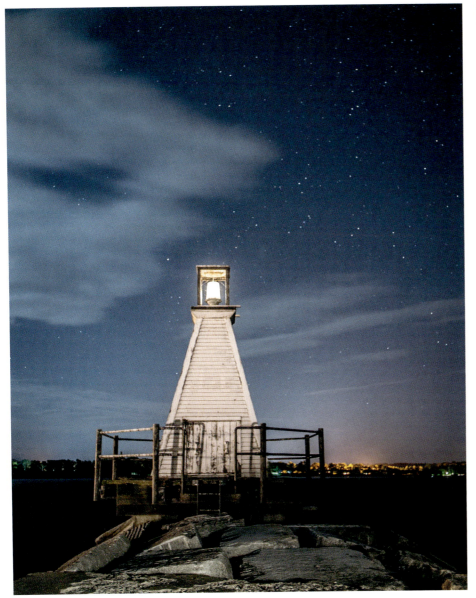

Burlington Harbor South, Burlington, Vermont

Spring Point Ledge, South Portland, Maine

Sankaty Head, Nantucket, Massachusetts

Marblehead, Ohio

Marshall Point, Port Clyde, Maine

Concord Point, Havre de Grace, Maryland

Minots Ledge, Cohasset, Massachusetts

Watch Hill, Rhode Island

Burnt Coat Harbor, Swan's Island, Maine *Dutch Island, Jamestown, Rhode Island*

Tchefuncte River, Madisonville, Louisiana

Fort Pickering, Salem, Massachusetts

Grindle Point, Islesboro, Maine *East Chop, Martha's Vineyard, Massachusetts*

Hendricks Head, Southport, Maine

Beavertail, Jamestown, Rhode Island

Execution Rocks, New Rochelle, New York

Robbins Reef, Bayonne, New Jersey

Round Island, Pascagoula, Mississippi

Patchogue Breakwater, Brookhaven, New York

Whitlocks Mill, Calais, Maine

Long Island, Boston, Massachusetts

Race Rock, Fishers Island, New York

Lighthouse Adventures

Page 10 left. Race Point Hiking to the Race Point Lighthouse is truly for those physically fit. While 4x4 rides are available certain times of the year, for most of us, getting here requires a strenuous mile-long hike. Perhaps the most challenging part is the soft sand that makes for a difficult walk. It's also a good idea to carry a handheld GPS to guide your return as many of the dune paths intersect making it quite easy to grow lost. First built in 1816, the original Race Point tower was replaced by the present one in 1876. The keeper's house is now a bed and breakfast run by the American Lighthouse Foundation. It's no coincidence having this lighthouse as the first image for *Portraits from the Dark* as it was the final image of the first book, and has switched roles with the Race Rock photographs. I thought it a nice idea to have both books sandwiched "between the Races," Race Point and Race Rock lighthouses. My good friend Sean Daly was with me on this shoot, and he clicked the shutter while I ran around lighting the scene with two stand lights and a flashlight.
Provincetown, Massachusetts, January 3, 2016, 7:27 p.m., 28°, 10-15mph wind
Nikon D4, 14mm lens, ISO 3200, f2.8, 25 secs
My thanks to Bob Trapani and the American Lighthouse Foundation, as well as the National Parks Service for guidance in accessing the lighthouse.

Cover,
Page 10 right. North This lighthouse is one of Rhode Island's gems, and I'm lucky to live so close. It's a pretty quick ferry ride from Point Judith to the island sitting about ten miles off Rhode Island's south coast. Several years before this adventure and early on in the project, I came here to capture the Milky Way for the first time. At that time, it was early in the Milky Way season. This particular night marked my second nighttime visit to the historic tower built in 1867. As the months move toward late summer, the galactic core becomes much more vertical and prominent. Earlier in the evening, we celebrated the opening of a gallery show of lighthouse images. It was clear with a new moon on the island's northern most point-- perfect conditions for a Stars & Lights photo-op!
Block Island, Rhode Island, August 7, 2015, 11:26 p.m., 65°, calm wind
Nikon D4, 14mm lens, ISO 3200, f2.8, 30 secs
North Light's grounds are open to the public, accessible by walking a half-mile beach to Sandy Point on Block Island.

Page 11 left. Thacher Island North Just off Rockport, Massachusetts' Cape Ann is a rare sight—an island adorned with two lighthouses, and most photographs show the lights together in the frame. I thought each deserved its own image. It took a number of tries over several months to land on the island, and it became a great lesson in perseverance and patience for the project. The first try was a dangerous late fall attempt with varying sea conditions, and Sean and I quickly learned to be more weather conscious moving forward. Seven months later, my daughter Amy and I completed the successful springtime trip, and also learned of seagulls' protective nature of their newborn offspring. Unwittingly, we landed at rooking time, with thousands of gulls and chicks everywhere. At one point, we had to swing sticks over our heads to keep the adult gulls from bombarding us. It was the beginning of the more dramatic Milky Way season, though its sky position was still more horizontal. Lighthouses have been on the island since 1771, and the current towers were built in 1861.
Rockport, Massachusetts, June 26, 2016, 11:23 p.m., 70°, 5-10mph wind
Nikon D4, 14mm lens, ISO 4000, f2.8, 25 secs
Paul St. Germain, with the Thacher Islands Association, was gracious in allowing us night access to the lighthouse, and Rockport Harbormaster, Rosemary Lesch, offered great tips on launching from the harbor.

Page 11 right. Eatons Neck On the north shore of New York's Long Island is a gated US Coast Guard rescue station off-limits to the general public. I received permission from the station chief to shoot the lighthouse at night. One of their personnel greeted me to be my guide, and he became my assistant for the evening shoot as we worked several angles of the lighthouse set among US Coast Guard housing. The lighthouse was constructed in 1799 and in the 1970s

was scheduled to be demolished, but local protests saved it from the wrecking ball.
Northport, New York, July 26, 2017, 10:05 p.m., 67°, calm wind
Nikon D4, 14mm lens, ISO 640, f2.8, 15 secs
This shoot was made possible by the US Coast Guard First District under Admiral Linda Fagan, and was completed with the help of Jared Esselman on the grounds of the station.

Page 12 left. Windmill Point Near the Canadian border in Northern Vermont sits this lighthouse on Lake Champlain. It is privately-owned by a family who also owns the nearby Isle la Motte Lighthouse. There were once a dozen lighthouses on the lake, and in the 1940s all were replaced by skeletal towers. In the early 2000s, the US Coast Guard demolished most of those towers, though for several, like Windmill Point, the beacons were placed back into the lighthouses. It was originally built on the point in 1830 and replaced in 1858.
Alburgh, Vermont, May 3, 2016, 10:08 p.m., 55°, calm wind
Nikon D4, 14mm lens, ISO 1600, f2.8, 25 secs
Rob Clarke was kind allowing the lighthouse access late at night and offered great advice for finding the best route to the point.

Page 12 right. Sleepy Hollow In this little hamlet along the Hudson River sits the Sleepy Hollow Lighthouse. It was built in 1883, though in its recent history, sat abandoned for several decades until locals relit it with a new acrylic Fresnel lens in 2015. It sits at the end of a town park and alongside a former General Electric manufacturing site being converted to high-end housing. This revitalization has breathed new life into the lighthouse neighborhood, and it can also be easily viewed from the new Gov. Mario Cuomo Memorial Bridge. The tripod had to be weighed down with sandbags to prevent the high winds from knocking it over on the night of my visit.
Tarrytown, New York, October 24, 2016, 7:25 p.m., 53°, 25-30mph wind
Nikon D4, 14mm lens, ISO 640, f2.8, 13 secs
The Sleepy Hollow Village administrator Anthony Giaccio was instrumental in keeping the park open late on the night of the shoot.

Page 13 left. Squirrel Point "Be careful of porcupines on your way out" were the last words of advice from the president of the foundation caring for this lighthouse along Maine's Kennebec River. He led me to a spot at the end of a road where a wooded path guides visitors to the lighthouse. It had been a fairly mild winter and the ground was mostly dry the night of my visit. The path winds through fairly thick woods, and the handheld GPS tracker kept my travels in check. The lighthouse was originally built in 1898 to warn vessels of a sharp bend in the river. I did not see any porcupines on this cold, winter night.
Arrowsic, Maine, January 12, 2016, 12:37 a.m., 20°, 5-10mph wind
Nikon D4, 14mm lens, ISO 2000, f3.2, 20 secs
Squirrel Point Lighthouse president Roman Wasilewski was helpful in finding the path to the lighthouse, as was his porcupine advice.

Page 13 right,
Page 152. Sandy Hook One issue frequently encountered in night lighthouse photography is access to lighthouses after sunset. Many National and State Parks close, and often lock their gates once darkness arrives, as is the case with Fort Hancock where this lighthouse is located. Sandy Hook is considered the oldest lighthouse in the country, and visits to it are mostly restricted to daylight hours. With Sean Daly assisting, we received permission to be on the grounds until 8pm, and our winter visit meant we only had a couple of hours to get our shots. Once we captured the standard images, we started searching for more unusual ones, and this angle shows some of the fortress surrounding the property. The tower is the original built in 1764, and is often part of the argument regarding the nation's oldest lighthouse. While Boston Lighthouse was the nation's first, its original building was destroyed by the British in the Revolutionary War in 1776, leaving Sandy Hook as the oldest remaining original lighthouse.

Highlands, New Jersey, March 2, 2017, 7:23 p.m., 41°, 15-20mph wind
Nikon D4, 14mm lens, ISO 1000, f2.8, 10 secs
The National Park Service rangers at Fort Hancock were instrumental in allowing us access to the grounds. My thanks to Pete McCarthy and Kimberly Pepper-Parks for their help.

Cover,
Page 14 left. Cove Point In 2018, the Stars & Lights project was adopted by the United States Lighthouse Society to continue its work on a national level. One of the first states we visited beyond the Northeast was Maryland, home to more than sixteen lighthouses. In the town of Lusby, are two lighthouses owned by the Calvert Maritime Museum, and they gave us permission to visit in early fall. It was unusually hot when we arrived for a daytime survey of the grounds, something we always like to do when possible. Arriving at night can sometimes lead to unexpected circumstances, making a daylight preview helpful. Later, after darkness set, we arrived and went about our work. One issue we hadn't noticed in the earlier survey was an extremely bright parking lot light high on a pole. Our inability to control the light forced us to avoid the front of the keeper's house. The backside, however, was darker and offered wonderful images of the majestic beacon against the stars. The lighthouse was established in 1828, and the US Coast Guard turned it over to the local county and to the Calvert Maritime Museum in 2000.
Lusby, Maryland, October 2, 2019, 10:30 p.m., 74°, 5-10mph wind
Nikon D4, 14mm lens, ISO 8000, f2.8, 3 secs
My thanks to Veronica Jordan from Drum Point Calvert Museum for giving us the late-night access to the beautiful lighthouse on the point. Sean Daly was my assistant on this trip to the Mid-Atlantic.

Page 14 right. Cape Elizabeth In the small town of Cape Elizabeth to the south of Portland, Maine are two lighthouse towers set high on a hill. Known as "Two Lights", they were built to work together as a range light for ships at sea. The rear tower was darkened years ago, but the front tower is still lighted. It is privately owned, and access to it is restricted. When I reached out to the homeowner, he enthusiastically allowed me to photograph it at night. I arrived on a rather warm winter night during a season of little snow. After shooting several angles on the property, I found this interesting window reflection with the stars glistening above the roofline. Erected in 1874, the lighthouse was famously depicted in an Edward Hopper painting in 1929.
Cape Elizabeth, Maine, February 3, 2016, 12:09 a.m., 28°, 20mph wind
Nikon D4, 14mm lens, 2000 ISO, f2.8, 25 secs
Lighthouse owners Bill and Nyssa Kourakos not only allowed access once, but also extended an open invitation for me to return to photograph future nighttime images.

Page 15 left. Barnegat Known affectionately as "Old Barney", this historic lighthouse, first established in 1835, was later replaced in 1859 as erosion threatened the original tower. It was an especially warm evening when I arrived at the lighthouse, located on a state park. Normally, each night the lighthouse is bathed in light and is much too bright for good star photography. The park agreed to extinguish the lights for me, which better enabled me to light the tower with my own instruments for better images. What couldn't be controlled was the excessive neighborhood ambient light reflecting off the heavy and humid summer air. I worked several other angles before finding this sweet reflection.
Barnegat Light Township, New Jersey, July 20, 2017, 10:16 p.m., 85°, calm wind
Nikon D4, 14mm lens, ISO 2000, f2.8, 20 secs
The Barnegat Lighthouse shoot took place with many thanks to Tom Keck, Cynthia Coritz, Diane Gormley and Ray Freas, and to the New Jersey Department of Environmental Protection.

Page 15 right. Fort Gratiot For about a year, my wife's work relocated her to Detroit, Michigan, and with it, offered me numerous opportunities to visit the state with the most lighthouses. The oldest lighthouse in Michigan is Fort Gratiot, at one time a US Coast Guard station on Lake Huron. It was built in 1829 and sits at the mouth of the St. Clair River, leading ships to Detroit. The park director graciously helped us with the logistics, and on the night of our shoot, the lake was frozen, though we weren't quite sure of the safety of the ice. With a line tied around my waist, I crawled onto the ice on all fours, fearful I might fall through. Don App, a US Coast Guard veteran, was my assistant for the night, and he held on tightly to the other end of the rope. To capture the reflection, I placed the camera directly onto the ice while still attached to the tripod. Don also acted as my lighting assistant, and aimed a dimmed LED light at the foreground ice chunks.
Port Huron, Michigan, January 17, 2018, 8:18 p.m., 22°, 10-15mph wind
Nikon D4, 14mm lens, ISO 640, f2.8, 8 secs
Dennis DeLor is greatly appreciated for allowing late night access to the grounds, and for selling my first book in the lighthouse gift shop.

Page 16 left. Sandy Neck This 1857 lighthouse on Cape Cod is a replacement for the original built in 1826. Now privately-owned, it was featured in a 2019 nationally televised heart medication commercial. I reached out to its owner as the Stars & Lights project was taking hold, and he granted permission for the nighttime visit. Driving to the barrier beach location was an option, though an expensive one. The charge for a beach driving permit is almost $200, so instead we launched the Whaler at the town dock and motored to the lighthouse. It was the height of the annual Perseid Meteor Shower, and the skies did not disappoint. The keeper's house is rented out during the summer, and the family staying there was notified of our visit plans. While we shot various angles, the family laid nearby in the sand watching the phenomenal shooting stars above. We had to be careful of huge poison ivy bushes surrounding the property. As we were about to motor away, we saw the lighthouse beacon reflecting off the water. It's always a bonus getting a reflection shot, and from the Whaler we deployed my custom 20-foot tripod to stabilized the camera.
Barnstable, Massachusetts, August 12, 2015, 10:48 p.m., 70°, 5mph wind
20-foot tripod, Nikon D4, 14mm, ISO 4000, f2.8, 25 secs
My thanks to Ken Morten for giving us permission to visit the lighthouse as well as providing his advice for accessing the barrier beach by boat rather than pay the town's 4x4 fee to drive there. Local Cape Cod photographer Tim Little joined me on this adventure.

Page 16 right. East Point If there is any lighthouse in the country in the direct bullseye to sea level rise, it's here in southern New Jersey. The beachhead adjacent to this lighthouse has all but disappeared in the new century, so in 2019, the state installed a synthetic berm to protect the lighthouse from the encroaching sea. I visited in 2017, and the dunes and seagrass visible then were now ripped away by a succession of winter storms, leaving the lighthouse extremely vulnerable. While a small group has been fighting for its protection and survival, the rising tides have placed the lighthouse in immediate peril. It's a shame this beautiful lighthouse, first built in 1849, may very well become a victim of the changing climate.
Maurice River Township, New Jersey, June 21, 2017, 10:52 p.m., 74°, 10-15mph wind
Nikon D4, 80-200mm lens at 180, ISO 2000, f2.8, 13 secs
East Point Lighthouse president Nancy Patterson Tidy has been a great resource for New Jersey lights, and has allowed me to stay on this property on several occasions while working on the collection.

Page 17 left. Biloxi In 2018, I was invited to present the Stars & Lights project to the United States Lighthouse Society convention in New Orleans. Figuring it would be a great time to shoot a few lighthouses, I started researching what I could capture while in the area. I landed in the city on the night of "Fat Tuesday," the final night of Mardi Gras, and reaching my hotel would be impossible during the celebratory parade in the middle of downtown. Instead, I drove east out of the airport to Mississippi and to its two remaining lighthouses. At one time, and over a century ago, there were eleven lighthouses in the state. I arrived in Biloxi shortly after its parade crowds cleared, but before the city had cleaned up the debris left by the party-goers. While the lighthouse is easy to shoot, doing so with stars is difficult given the amount of direct light from multiple streetlights. The lighthouse is located on the median of a four-lane highway running along the Gulf shores. It opened in 1849 and in 2009, was commemorated on a United States postage stamp.

Biloxi, Mississippi, February 13, 2018, 11:43 p.m., 67°, no wind
Nikon D4, 14mm lens, ISO 50, f5.6, 8 secs
The Biloxi Lighthouse is in the center of Beach Boulevard and publicly accessible.

Page 17 right. Huntington Harbor For several years, this wonderful lighthouse, in the middle of Hunting Harbor on New York's Long Island, had undergone an extensive renovation. What started as a simple foundation repair brought discoveries of major structural issues, and for a time, the lighthouse's survival was at stake. The project took a number of years to complete, and for most of the time, heavy construction equipment was placed around the lighthouse, making artistic photography impossible. It coincided with the acquisition of many of the images for the first Stars & Lights book, but in the summer of 2018, we finally made it to the harbor. We traveled to New York for what was predicted to be a clear night, but clouds soon filtered over the harbor during our visit. The lighthouse was built in 1912, replacing a land-based one built in 1857. In 1985, it was slated by the US Coast Guard to be razed, but local opposition and a newly formed foundation saved it from demolition.
Huntington Harbor, New York, July 11, 2018, 11 p.m., 73°, no wind
Nikon D4, 14mm lens, ISO 320, f2.8, 15 secs
I immediately made a connection with Huntington Lighthouse president Pam Setchell on many different levels; we're both photographers, boaters, and lighthouse presidents. She has proved a valued resource for USA Stars & Lights. Sean Daly was my assistant for the shoot.

Page 18 left. Point Judith On a clear beautiful summer night, I ran out to shoot a couple of lighthouses local to me. Earlier, I made arrangements with the Watch Hill Lighthouse to be on its property, and there I grabbed some wonderful images. While heading home, I would pass near the Point Judith Lighthouse, and I called the station at the last minute to see if I could get onto the property. It's an active US Coast Guard rescue station and closed to the public. The duty officer was familiar with the project, and buzzed me in. Approaching the tower, I noticed the interior stairway lights were on, something I'd never seen before. I took advantage of their presence as they would add an interesting element to the image. There's often an exterior floodlight on the nearby oil house that hits the tower, so I reached up and unscrewed the bulb, which then resulted in beautiful rays from the stairway light hitting the grass. Off in the distant horizon is the Sakonnet Lighthouse beacon. The current Point Judith tower is a replacement built in 1857 for the original 1810 lighthouse. That tower was destroyed by a hurricane in 1815.
Narragansett, Rhode Island, June 29, 2014, 11:51 p.m., 62°, 10 mph wind
Nikon D4, 17-35mm lens at 17, ISO 2000, f2.8, 15 secs
I appreciate the great support from US Coast Guard Chief Eric Barruzzi (now retired,) who was in charge at Pt. Judith at the time of this shoot.

Page 18 right. Southwest Ledge I'm pretty sure the streak in the sky in this image is the lights of the International Space Station during a long exposure of this lighthouse off New Haven. It was built in 1876 to guide ships into the harbor. With my brother Jack assisting, we arrived on the jetty after splashing our Boston Whaler at a city boat ramp about a half-mile away. Jack stayed offshore in the Whaler and lit the tower, and I spent about an hour shooting different angles. While later editing the images, I noticed the strange line in only one frame. It's the first time I'd captured the station while photographing a lighthouse.
New Haven, Connecticut, August 26, 2016, 9:25 p.m., 83°, calm wind
Nikon D4 14mm lens, ISO 640, f2.8, 20 secs
I appreciate the New Haven Parks Department and Sabrina Bruno for their suggestion to use the Lighthouse Point boat ramp for the shoot.

Page 19 left. Piney Point As the project continued growing on the national stage, trips further outside of the Northeast were warranted. With Sean Daly assisting, we took an early fall drive to the Mid-Atlantic to begin capturing those states' lights. This lighthouse was first built in 1836 and sits at the mouth of the Potomac River at the northern point of the Chesapeake Bay. We received permission to shoot on the grounds at night, but had to cover several LED fixtures that shone too brightly on the tower, and replace them with our own, more photogenic lights. The most concerning issue here is the lights from a nearby fuel depot

that infiltrated the night sky, making our star capturing ability low. On this night, clouds also filtered into the area, further complicating the shoot.
Piney Point, Maryland, October 2, 2019, 9:02 p.m., 84°, no wind
Nikon D4, 14mm lens, ISO 1000, f2.8, 5 secs
My thanks to April Havens at the St. Mary's County Parks and Recreation Museum Division for allowing us access to the lighthouse at night.

Page 19 right. Avery Point Early in the project and long before the realization these photographs were becoming an important collection, I was quickly running out of Rhode Island subjects. My sights turned to the Connecticut lighthouses to the west of where we live. One of the more accessible lighthouses is one of the last built by the US Coast Guard in the United States in 1944. It sits on what is now the University of Connecticut's Avery Point campus. You can park fairly close and take a short walk to the tower. Night shooting is easy as this lighthouse is well-lit by several high intensity floodlights, however, the bright lights make star capturing really difficult. I ventured around to the darker water-side and away from the lights, where I then captured some nice images. I found a frozen tidal pool on the top of a large rock, close to the water's edge, which created this wonderful reflection that looks much more complicated than it actually was.
Groton, Connecticut, January 22, 2015, 11:59 p.m., 28°, 5-10mph wind
Nikon D4 17-35mm lens at 17, ISO 1250, f2.8, 25 secs
A thank you to Jim Streeter for advice about Avery Point. The lighthouse is on the grounds of the University of Connecticut's Marine Services Southeastern Branch and is publicly accessible.

Page 20 left. Horton Point The town of Southold, New York has eight lighthouses with seven of them still lit. A town museum is in the Horton Point Lighthouse, and I contacted officials for their permission to shoot after dark. It's a short drive to the New London ferry from my home, and this late fall day was perfect weather for the ride across Long Island Sound. I arrived in late afternoon, and once darkness came, had about an hour to shoot before I'd need to leave to catch the last ferry back to Connecticut. What I didn't expect was to have four bright security lights come on at each corner of the building. There was no one around to help turn them off, so I searched the grounds, found a ladder, climbed up, and covered the two spotlights nearest the building's main entrance. I've taught a few television lighting classes at the Rhode Island School of Design, and often say the three rules of lighting are "control, control, control". Without control, good photography is impossible. Sometimes it takes drastic measures to achieve the best results. The lighthouse was built in 1857 to help vessels navigate Long Island Sound.
Southold, New York, November 17, 2016, 6:49 p.m., 55°, 10-15mph wind
Nikon D4, 14mm lens, ISO 2000, f2.8, 13 secs
My thanks to Karen Lund from the town of Southold for the permission, and to keeper Patrick Haggerty for allowing the night photography.

Page 20 right. Castle Hill Since 1823, a lighthouse has been on the grounds here, though this one is a replacement built in 1842. It sits a few miles from my home, and is pretty convenient to swing by when it's a peak meteor time. In December, if it's clear, the Geminids are usually easy to catch, if you are lucky. While walking to the lighthouse from the parking lot, dozens of shooting stars were visible in the skies above. I placed an LED light on a stand uphill from the lighthouse to bring out its finer details. Once the camera was set, I simply waited for a meteor to blast through the frame. It can be frustrating to see an entire sky above filled with small individual light streaks but not be able to capture them in the camera frame. It's also unusual to see a shooting star while capturing it at the same moment. In most cases, at least for me, when I've discovered one in a photograph, it's usually after the fact when editing the images. On this night, I actually saw the one captured in this image and Lady Luck was on my side!
Newport, Rhode Island, December 14, 2018, 2:11 a.m., 22°, 5-10mph wind
Nikon D4, 14mm lens, 5000, ISO, f2.8, 20 secs

Introduction Page 3. Castle Hill NEOWISE Comet In March 2020, NASA's Near-Earth Object Wide-field Infrared Survey Explorer (NEOWISE) discovered a comet racing through our solar system. As it grew closer to Earth, it started appearing in the night skies, and lasted for about three weeks in the summer of 2020.

It made sense to try and capture it with a lighthouse, and Castle Hill is only about 20 minutes from my home. In fact, from the angle of this image, my home is located somewhere in the vicinity directly underneath the comet, though not on the water. I had to hike from a parking lot to the lighthouse, then scamper over the rocks to get the best vantage point of the two objects juxtaposed in the frame.
Newport, Rhode Island, July 15, 2020 10:09 p.m., 70°, slight breeze
Nikon D4, 80-200 lens at 80mm, 4000 ISO, f8, 20 secs
The lighthouse is on the grounds of the Inn at Castle Hill and its accessibility is allowed for those visiting the hotel. Photography of the lighthouse, however, is not discouraged.

Page 21 left. Long Point;
Page 21 right. Wood End While few lighthouses are grouped together within this collection, there are some exceptions. These two on the end of the Cape Cod peninsula are almost identical and were captured on the same night early in the project. I'd expanded east from my Rhode Island home to capture Massachusetts' lights, and made the two-hour trip to the end of Route 6 on the Cape. It is there at a circular parking lot where the real adventure begins. A mile-long jetty, the Provincetown Causeway, leads to the barrier beach and dunes where both lighthouses are located about a half-mile from each other. Crossing the jetty must be timed on the tides because at high tide, much of it is underwater. On this visit, I arrived at low tide while it was on the way in, and during the return to the parking lot, it was on its way out. You cannot cross the jetty at high tide or you risk being swept away by the water. I made my way to Long Point by walking in the tidal flats as the water came up behind me. (If you look at the Memorial page at the front of the book, you'll see a tidal flats photograph taken on this same night.) The present Long Point Lighthouse was built in 1875 replacing the original tower built in 1827. Its design was identical to the Wood End Lighthouse constructed three years earlier. In the Long Point image, you can see the red light of Wood End in the background. Long Point is more in the direct line of the lights from Provincetown, while Wood End is shielded by the dunes.
Provincetown, Massachusetts, April 15, 2015, 68°, calm wind
Long Point-9:55 p.m., Nikon 14mm lens, ISO 2000, f2.8, 25 secs
Wood End-11:20 p.m., Nikon 14mm lens, ISO 4000, f2.8, 25 secs
The lighthouses are on the Cape Cod National Seashore and are publicly accessible.

Page 22 left. Tongue Point Few realize this distinctive black lighthouse, built in 1895, is in the middle of Bridgeport, Connecticut. As you speed by on I-95 near the power plant, the lighthouse is visible if only momentarily. It sits on a peninsula near the plant's pier, and is off-limits to the public. It can also be viewed while on the ferry to Long Island whose docks are adjacent to the lighthouse. I received permission from the plant's parent company to visit the lighthouse at night, and had to request they turn off a string of security lights that interrupt star capture. Shooting here was a pivotal point in the project as I discovered the absence of night lighthouse photographs while researching Tongue Point. While searching for images of this lighthouse, I could find none from nighttime, convincing me that this project needed attention.
Bridgeport, Connecticut, May 8, 2015, 9:40 p.m., 64°, calm wind
Nikon D4, 17-35 lens at 17, ISO 400, f 2.8, 15 secs
Many thanks to PSEG's Melissa Ficuciello for the access, and to Tom Corpus for controlling the lights on the night of the visit.

Page 22 right. Edgartown Harbor Originally built in 1828, the present tower is a replacement constructed in 1881. This lighthouse leads ships in and out of Edgartown Harbor on Martha's Vineyard, Massachusetts. During my professional career, I've worked as a freelance network cameraman for forty years, and on this night, I received a last-minute call to work on the island for a couple of late night live shots. As it was a new moon with forecasts calling for clear skies, I grabbed the still gear on my way out the door to catch the ferry. On both nights, the television shoots were finished around midnight, allowing the perfect opportunity to capture four of the island's five lighthouses. They were the first images of the project outside of my home state of Rhode Island, and it happened months before I realized how important this project was to become. The satellite truck operator was my assistant on this night, and under my direction, he light-painted the scene for some of the images. (Light-painting is a process of filling a scene with light, usually from a flashlight, to illuminate the film plane of the camera.) As it sits near the center of town with many other light sources, the ambient illumination kept the star count down, but the strength of the summertime Milky Way cut through much of the light pollution.

Edgartown, Massachusetts, July 30, 2014, 2 a.m., 68°, calm wind
Nikon D4, 17-35mm lens at 17, ISO 3200, f2.8, 20 secs

The Edgartown Lighthouse is located on the beachhead near the harbor and is publicly accessible. Satellite truck operator Chris Larose assisted on this night.

Page 23 left. Cleveland Ledge Once the project was underway, I found it difficult shooting lighthouses offshore or not located on islands. I hired a welder friend to create a 20-foot water-based tripod to access those that might not otherwise be photographed. We've shot about a dozen unique images with the tripod. Off West Falmouth, Massachusetts, in thirty-five feet of water, is the Cleveland Ledge Lighthouse. It's too deep to use the tripod, and the nearest land is more than two miles away. Clearly, the only possible imagery would have to take place on the lighthouse itself. It's also privately owned, and only accessible with the help of a special US Coast Guard ladder. I received permission to visit from the owner, and the US Coast Guard was kind enough to let us borrow the ladder to complete the mission. We launched the Whaler from a town boat ramp and took headed due west to the lighthouse. For this image, I shined a flashlight through a window onto an interior wall to illuminate the inside. The Milky Way made a beautiful appearance over the lighthouse, built in 1944, on this midsummer night. It is the last official US Coast Guard lighthouse constructed in the country.

Falmouth, Massachusetts, August 2, 2016, 10:11 p.m., 68°, 5-10mph wind
Nikon D4, 14mm lens, ISO 4000, f2.8, 25 secs

The lighthouse is distantly visible from West Falmouth. Thank you to owner Sandy Boyd for access, and to the Woods Hold US Coast Guard ATON office for the use of its ladder. My friend Eddy Stahowiak assisted on this adventure.

Page 23 right. Absecon Sometimes this project can be frustrating regarding weather uncertainties. With a new moon and a forecast of clear skies, I set out from Rhode Island for New Jersey and an appointment to meet a board member of this lighthouse in Atlantic City, New Jersey. It was a beautiful early fall day and the ride was uneventful, though a little long. After nearly five hours, the shoreline came into view from the parkway. So, too, did a large fog bank. It looked as though it would remain offshore, but while crossing over the causeway to the barrier island where the city is located, my heart sank. It led directly into the fog. At the time, I was under deadline for the first book, and wanted to get the lighthouse image for it. The board member unlocked the front gate, and I had the run of the grounds for about an hour. The lighthouse sits among a few homes with the casinos only a few blocks away. There is direct light all around, and capturing stars under clear skies would be a challenge. In a way, the fog made the photography easier in that I needn't worry about the stars. The lighthouse was opened in 1857 and is the tallest in New Jersey. It was deactivated as an aid to navigation in 1933 and is now a private aid to navigation.

Atlantic City, New Jersey, September 25, 2017, 8:21 p.m., 68°, 10-15mph wind
Nikon D4, 14mm lens, ISO 800, f2.8, 1/5th sec

Thank you to Executive Director Jean Muchanic for the access and to board member Ruth Latorre for unlocking the gate on the night of my visit.

Page 24 left. Stratford Shoal We splashed the Whaler in Stratford Harbor, Connecticut on a pleasant summer night, for the seven-mile ride to this lighthouse. It sits exactly in the middle of Long Island Sound and is often called "Middle Ground Lighthouse". At the time of the visit, the lighthouse was up for auction and quite close to being sold to a lighthouse hotelier who hoped to transform it into a bed and breakfast. He won the auction, but failed to get bank financing as the government couldn't create a title for the property due to technicalities. It's a shame because the place could really use some care and maintenance. As we pulled the boat up to the light, the lower rungs of the access ladder were terribly damaged by years of storms. All were bent to a 45° angle, making for a really difficult climb. Once on the gangway, I could see several missing windows as well as missing railings. It's a beautiful building, originally built in 1877 and resembles the Race Rock on the east end of the Sound. I shot various angles while Sean remained offshore lighting the scene from the Whaler.

Stratford, Connecticut, July 6, 2016, 10:08 p.m., 68°, 5-10mph wind
Nikon D4, 14mm lens, ISO2000, f3.5, 20 secs
At the time of the shoot, Nick Korstad was about to take ownership of the lighthouse from the government, and I'd received his permission to visit the lighthouse. That sale fell through, and the lighthouse is still government-owned. Many thanks to Nick for his dream of owning this gothic-designed structure.

Page 24 right. Nauset This is one of the more popular lighthouses to photograph in Massachusetts and is easily accessible in the National Seashore Park. With a forecast of clear skies and new moon, it was a quick drive for me to the lighthouse on Cape Cod. It was the end of the year's Milky Way season, a time when the galactic core is still visible, but not as strong as months earlier. The lighthouse was built 1877 as one of the original twin towers at Chatham, but in 1923, was moved due to erosion. It was again moved in 1996 to its present location.
Eastham, Massachusetts, October 7, 2015, 9:47 p.m., 62°, calm winds
Nikon D4, 17-35 lens at 35, ISO 3200, f2.8, 25 secs
The lighthouse is publicly accessible along the shores of the Cape Cod National Seashore.

Page 25 left. Ludington North Breakwater Life circumstances had us spending a lot of time in Detroit, Michigan in 2018, and I took advantage. I reached out to the foundation running four lighthouses on Lake Michigan, and soon, a late winter shoot in Ludington occurred. There are two lights in the town, Big Sable and Ludington North Breakwater, and we shot both on the same night. The latter requires a long walk on a concrete pier to reach the lighthouse. We were fortunate that a recent warm spell had melted the ice previously encasing the pier. Had we been shooting a week earlier, it's likely the ice would have made the attempt too dangerous. My assistant for the night was Don App, a US Coast Guard veteran. He stayed on the beach and aimed a high-powered LED light at the tower while I shot from the breakwater. The lighthouse was built in 1871, with a hull-like design to protect it from lake ice floes.
Ludington, Michigan, March 11, 2018, 10:55 p.m., 28°, no wind
Nikon D4, 14mm lens, ISO 2000, f2.8, 13 secs
The Sable Points Lighthouse Keepers Association owns and operates several Michigan lighthouses, and its president Pete Manting was particularly supportive allowing access to all on several different occasions. The Ludington North Breakwater Lighthouse is publicly accessible through a lengthy walk out on the town breakwater.

Page 25 right. Sodus Bay In the town of Sodus, New York, along Lake Ontario, are two lighthouses about a half-mile apart. The Sodus Bay Museum Light is land-based along the lakeshore, and this one is on a pier off the town's beach. I took a long drive from Rhode Island on a warm, early spring day to reach the town, and went to work shortly after sunset. The warmth of the day turned colder as darkness settled, and a crowded parking lot grew quiet. I walked out to the lighthouse and set an LED light on a stand at the bend in the pier. A curious local photographer started inquiring about my process and soon became my assistant for the shoot. In the 1800s, twin towers once stood guiding ships into the harbor. The present tower was erected on the pier in 1938.
Sodus Point, New York, April 23, 2017, 9:49 p.m., 64°, no wind
Nikon D4, 14mm lens, ISO 3200, f2.8, 25 secs
The Sodus Outer Lighthouse is located on a jetty off the town beach and is publicly accessible.

Page 26 left. Old Saybrook Breakwater In this southern Connecticut town are two lighthouses sitting about a half-mile apart from each other, settled in among mansions in an exclusive neighborhood called Fenwick. Until her death in 2003, actress Katherine Hepburn had a summer home here. For many years, the US Coast Guard housed personnel in the Lynde Point Lighthouse, and just south of it, along the Connecticut River, is the Old Saybrook Breakwater Lighthouse. It's known for being depicted on a Connecticut state license plate. Built in 1886, it was one of the first cast-iron lights in the country. I ventured out on the jetty after shooting the Lynde Point Lighthouse, though it was early in the project and before I'd purchased proper safety equipment for the adventures. In retrospect, it was a pretty foolish risk to take—walking out alone on a jetty surrounded by cold tidal water, in the dark, with no safety gear on a freezing winter night. What

could go wrong? Luckily, nothing on this night, but it gave pause and within a few days, I would properly gear up to be better prepared in the future.
Old Saybrook, Connecticut, January 23, 2015, 1:34 a.m., 28°, 10-15mph wind
Nikon D4, 17-35mm lens at 17, ISO 1250, f2.8, 25 secs
My appreciation to the New Haven US Coast Guard office allowing access to their two properties along the Connecticut River. Since the shoot, the Old Saybrook Breakwater Lighthouse has been sold to a private owner.

Page 26 right. Thacher Island South Another lesson in preparedness came with the Thacher Island Lighthouses. First established in 1771, the only remaining twin towers in the U.S. are on the island. In the fall of 2016, Sean and I accepted as fact, a forecast calling for 10-15mph westerly winds off Rockport, Massachusetts. We splashed the Whaler in the sheltered harbor, and as we motored outside of the mooring field, the winds shifted from the north. As we approached the island, wind speeds picked up to 20-25, pushing swells over the bow of the boat. Within a hundred feet of the island, in worsening conditions, we decided to abort the mission. Seven months later, I returned to the island with my daughter Amy assisting, and things were much improved. However, we didn't realize the boat ramp was as slick as ice from marine growth. Each step was filled with anxiety as both of us were sliding back down the ramp to the water. It took several minutes to make it up the thirty feet to the drier area with better footing.
Rockport, Massachusetts, June 26, 2016, 10:53 p.m., 70°, 5-10mph wind
Nikon D4, 14mm lens, ISO 3200, f2.8, 25 secs
Thanks again to Paul St. Germain with the Thacher Islands Association in allowing us night access of the lighthouse.

Page 27 left. Portsmouth Harbor At the entrance to Portsmouth Harbor, New Hampshire, on Fort Constitution sits this lighthouse, first established in 1771. The current tower is a rebuild finished in 1878. It's part of an active US Coast Guard station, and I received permission to be on the base after sunset. I was assigned two rescue swimmers who quickly and eagerly became my assistants for the night, and I gave them a lesson in light-painting. That's a process where a photographer opens the camera shutter and "paints" with light, usually a flashlight, while the image is exposed onto the film plane. With my camera, it's burned onto its digital sensor.
Portsmouth, New Hampshire, November 4, 2015, 7:49 p.m., 52°, light wind
Nikon D4, 14mm lens, ISO 2500, f2.8, 25 secs
Thank you to Lighthouse president Jeremy D'Entremont for help in allowing the nighttime access to the property, and to the US Coast Guard Station Portsmouth Harbor and rescue swimmers Joe Cea and Devin Greenwell for their assistance the night of the shoot.

Page 27 right. Nubble Arguably one of the most photographed lighthouses in the country, Nubble Lighthouse first opened in 1879 and is owned by the Town of York. It is easily seen from a parking lot across the gap from the island where it sits. While the island is off-limits, the parking lot is at the end of a public road, and one can simply pull up in a car to see the lighthouse. You don't even need to get out to capture a memorable image. In warmer months, night photography is made difficult by a bright LED light on the front of the property. I was in the area for television business on a warm February evening, and the front light was off for the season. Other than the beacon, the lighthouse was dark, and I lit the entire setting with a single LED light placed on a stand at the edge of the parking lot.
Cape Neddick, York, Maine, February 21, 2017, 8:14 p.m., 38°, calm wind
Nikon D4, 14mm lens, ISO 2000, f2.8, 20 secs
Nubble Lighthouse is publicly viewable from the town park on a point in York, Maine.

Page 28 left. Lynde Point In 2015, as the lighthouse captures started to grow, the need to expand to neighboring states was apparent. Less than an hour's drive from my home are four easily reachable Connecticut lights, though all have varying degrees of accessibility. Lynde Point is a US Coast Guard property, formerly used as personnel housing, but vacant at the time of my visit. I reached out to the local command staff to obtain permission to be on the property at night. It sits on the edge of an exclusive community along the Connecticut River where posted signs warn against illegal entry. I parked in the driveway and made the short

walk to the backyard facing the river. At the time, I was lighting most of the shoots by "light-painting" with a flashlight, and managed some interesting angles of Lynde Point. This image was taken only after shooting the nearby Old Saybrook Breakwater Light, and while on the return walk along the beachfront, where I saw the reflection in the moist sand. The Lynde Point Lighthouse was first established in 1802 and the present tower was finished in 1838.
Old Saybrook, Connecticut, January 23, 2015, 2:19 a.m., 28°, calm wind
Nikon D4, 17-35mm lens at 17, ISO 1000, f2.8, 25 secs
Thanks to the US Coast Guard station in New Haven for the access to the lighthouse.

Page 28 right. Ten Pound Island On a small island in the middle of Gloucester Harbor, Massachusetts, sits this little lighthouse. It was early on in the project, and before I learned the importance of having an assistant on most shoots. I pulled the Whaler from my Rhode Island home to the town launch near the local high school. It was a short trip to the island, and the tide was really low. I had studied satellite photos of the island and thought a landing might be close to the lighthouse, but at low tide and in darkness, everything looked different. I beached the boat in the sand, and set the anchor for the coming rising tide. There were no apparent paths I could find in the darkness to reach the lighthouse, so I had to cut through the brambles. Once I reached the light, my clothing and camera gear were covered in round thorny weeds from the brush. There were hundreds of them, but I left them knowing there'd be more collected on the return. It was a quiet night of solitude on the island with the historic 1821 tower, allegedly named for the amount of money settlers paid native tribes for its purchase.
Gloucester, Massachusetts, November 9, 2015, 7:10 p.m., 58°, calm wind
Nikon D4, 14mm lens, ISO 2000, f2.8, 20 secs
The lighthouse is on a town-owned island in the middle of Gloucester Harbor and is accessible by boat or kayak.

Page 29 left. Fenwick Island This was our first lighthouse photographed as we began the project expansion into the Mid-Atlantic. I was pleasantly surprised to find some stars over the tower because the entire scene is bathed in direct light from neighborhood street lights and houses. Built in 1858, it is the oldest lighthouse in Delaware. It was turned over to the State in 1982 and now run by a private foundation. On the night of our visit, the keeper's house and tower were surrounded by the construction fencing of a renovation company. We knew there'd be ambient and direct lighting issues here, and pretty much had sworn off catching stars. Next door to the property is a private home, and behind it is a trailer park. The neighborhood is in the middle of a barrier beach with the Atlantic to the east and a bay to the west. On the north side of the lighthouse is Delaware; on the south side is Maryland. Out in front is a streetlight shining directly onto the house and the tower, but the north side is shielded and a fairly dark area can be found. We lit the neighboring house with an LED light on a stand, and felt fortunate to capture the stars above on an exceptionally warm, early fall evening.
Fenwick Island, Delaware, October 1, 2019, 8:11 p.m., 74°, no wind
Nikon D4, 14mm lens, ISO 250, f2.8, 13 secs
The lighthouse is in the middle of a crowded neighborhood on a barrier island and is publicly accessible. Sean Daly was along for this trip.

Page 29 right. Bluff Point This 1874 lighthouse on Lake Champlain, New York, underwent an extensive renovation in 2014. For many years, all of the lake's lighthouse beacons were removed and placed on skeletal towers. In the early 2000s, realizing most of the towers were crumbling, the US Coast Guard returned the lights into many of the lighthouses. I met the keeper at a dock for the short boat ride to the island where the lighthouse sits. We arrived at sunset, when the keeper gave us a tour of the grounds and lighthouse. With its substantial renovation completed, the lighthouse is once again a beautiful property. It sits high on a hill and is a source of newfound pride for locals.
Valcour Island, Peru, New York, August 24, 2016, 9:08 p.m., 77°, 5-10mph wind
Nikon D4, 14mm lens, ISO1250, f2.8, 20 secs
The help of keeper Roger Harwood is greatly appreciated here at Bluff Point. He not only gave me a ride to the island on his pontoon boat, but also gave an insightful tour of the lighthouse prior to the shoot. He then assisted with the lighting.

Page 30 left. Stepping Stones On a sparkling early fall evening, Sean and I visited three lighthouses in the western flank of Long Island Sound. We splashed the Whaler in Greenwich Harbor before motoring eleven miles to this 1877 lighthouse located off the United States Merchant Marine Academy at King's Point, New York. While the chart says the bottom here is rocky, we found launching our special 20-foot tripod quite easy as the seafloor turned out to be sandy. That was a relief because setting the tripod on rocks can be problematic. We arrived at sunset and had a generator and electric grill with us to have a cookout while waiting for darkness to set. After capturing our images at Stepping Stones, we continued our evening's quest by shooting the relatively close Execution Rocks and Great Captain Island Lighthouses.
North Hempstead, New York, September 22, 2016, 8:43 p.m., 84°, calm wind
20-foot tripod, Nikon D4, 14mm lens, ISO 250, f2.8, 15 secs
The lighthouse is located off the US Merchant Marine Academy at King's Point, and can be distantly seen from the Throgs Neck Bridge in New York City. It is accessible only by boat.

Page 30 right. Borden Flats This image was another special "get" as few have ever photographed the lighthouse here as we managed to achieve. With my daughter Amy assisting, we launched the Whaler about a mile upstream on the Taunton River. The shoot was planned for low tide, and the chart said we'd find an area with fourteen feet of depth south of the tower. We set the custom tripod for seventeen feet, and the legs settled nicely into the sandy river bottom. The difficulty here was photographing stars as the bridge and city both throw off large amounts of direct light. The lighthouse opened in 1881 and today operates as a bed and breakfast.
Fall River, Massachusetts, June 21, 2015, 11:52 p.m., 73°, calm wind
20-foot tripod, Nikon D4, 17-35mm lens at 17, ISO 250, f2.8, 20 secs
The privately-owned lighthouse operates as a bed and breakfast. It is accessible only by boat.

Page 31 left. Sandy Point This lighthouse, located on an island on Rhode Island's Narragansett Bay, was originally located in Newport, and later moved to this location in 1851. Early in the project, I motored alone to the island for its capture. I grabbed a nearby mooring and rowed the inflatable dinghy ashore. I mistakenly left it too close to the shore, and foolishly didn't pay any mind to the tide: it was rising. I've been a long-time boater, and occasionally have made some dumb moves, but this one rates pretty high. I failed to set the inflatable's anchor, while getting "in the zone" shooting the lighthouse, and then forgot to check on the dinghy. When I finally did, it was floating away offshore on the rising tide. In the next twenty minutes, I ran up and down the beach, looking for anything to help, stole a kayak, was caught then forgiven, and finally retrieved the dinghy for the return to my boat following the completion of my shoot.
Prudence Island, Rhode Island, June 2, 2014, 11:42 p.m., 52°, calm wind
Nikon D4, 17-35mm lens at 17, ISO 800, f2.8, 25 secs
The lighthouse is publicly accessible on Prudence Island.

Page 31 right. North Pier Located in an Erie, Pennsylvania state park are two historic and very different lighthouses. While the nearby Presque Island Lighthouse was easily accessible near the park road, this lighthouse was located at the end of a pier so as to lead ships to the harbor. I met up with a local photographer to assist me on this cold winter night, and we made our way out onto the pier. At the end near the lighthouse, there was thick ice on which to venture to get a nice side angle of the historic tower. We lit it from the beach with an LED light on a stand. Since 1830, there's been a lighthouse on the pier though its location has been moved several times. The present tower was built in 1857.
Erie, Pennsylvania, March 4, 2018, 9:18 p.m., 28°, 5-10mph wind
Nikon D4, 14mm lens, ISO 800, f4, 15 secs
A chance meeting with local artist Heather Hertel at the United States Lighthouse Society convention in New Orleans led to the several Erie shoots. It then led to an introduction to Mike Kohler, who was vitally important to a successful night of shooting on the Presque Isle peninsula. My thanks to both for their great help.

Page 32 left. Romer Shoal During Super Storm Sandy in 2012, several lighthouses near New York Harbor were either damaged or destroyed by the tidal surge. Old Orchard Shoal Light was knocked over by the powerful wave, and this nearby lighthouse almost met a similar fate. During the storm, its jetty was rearranged, the porch decking and roof were ripped off, and its front door was torn away. Yet, the lighthouse survived. We received permission from its owner for our night visit, and we hired a captain and boat out of Staten Island to bring us to the lighthouse south of the Verrazzano Narrows Bridge. He dropped us off at the lighthouse ladder. My son Cory assisted from directly on the lighthouse, while his friend Andy Romer (no relation to the lighthouse) lighted the scene from the boat. We carefully made our way down to the jetty remnants, but had difficulty maneuvering over the rocks to a safe shooting point. With the boulders all scattered about, we were lucky to have a low tide during our visit. It was harrowing and dangerous, which forced our time on the slippery rocks to be short. The lighthouse originally opened in 1898, but now its future is in jeopardy as little has been done to repair Sandy's damage.
Ambrose Channel, New Jersey, August 16, 2017, 11:18 p.m., 82°, calm winds
Nikon D4, 14mm lens, ISO 1000, f2.8, 13 secs
My thanks to Keith Kilcannon for the permission for us to land on the rocks of the lighthouse for the shoot. Thanks also Capt. Gary Toske, Teresa Salerno, and Glen Miller from Miller's Launch on Staten Island for safely getting us on and off the lighthouse.

Page 32 right. Sakonnet This was the final lighthouse left to shoot in Rhode Island, and it took nearly two years to accomplish. It sits on rocks in the open Atlantic Ocean waters, making access quite difficult. With a team of four, we motored from my town to the lighthouse located off Little Compton. Sean Daly and I took the inflatable to the site, while my neighbor Keith Finck piloted the boat, and with our friend and fellow photographer Richard Kizirian, stayed offshore to light the scene. We had trouble finding a safe landing spot until we discovered stairs had been chiseled into the rock with cleats positioned alongside. We tied off the dinghy and made our way to the lighthouse. It was built on the rocks in 1884, and survived many hurricanes and Nor'easters. Sean used a flashlight on the foreground while Richard hit the tower with the LED light from the boat. We finished our images, but seas had increased since our landing, making for a harrowing return to the boat.
Little Compton, Rhode Island, June 7, 2015, 9:51 p.m., 58°, 10-15mph wind
Nikon D4, 14mm lens, ISO 2000, f2.8, 20 secs
Thanks to harbormaster Mike Massa and Sakonnet Lighthouse President Scott Brown for permission, but also tips for landing on the rock.

Page 33 left. Livingstone Memorial For almost a year, my wife's job brought her to working in Detroit, Michigan. It offered a great opportunity to shoot lighthouses whenever I'd visit, which was often. In the middle of the Detroit River is a large island and park, though much of it had been lately suffering from neglect. The lighthouse was built in 1930 as a memorial to a man instrumental in bringing shipping to the Great Lakes. My friend and US Coast Guard veteran, Don App, assisted on this cold and windy winter night. We made the long walk to the lighthouse from the parking lot. Once there, we lit the tower with an LED light on a stand, and used a second one for the foreground grass. The grounds are open to the public, though they were quite deserted on this night. Off in the distance was the city skyline.
Detroit, Michigan, January 18, 2018, 8:45 p.m. 26°, 20-25mph wind
Nikon D4, 14mm lens, ISO 200, f2.8, 10 secs
The lighthouse is accessible on a public park on Detroit's Belle Isle.

Page 33 right. Turtle Rock Nestled among boathouses along Philadelphia's Schuylkill River is Turtle Rock Lighthouse, built in 1897 to help coal ships navigate a large river curve. About a decade later, an athletic association, the Sedgeley Club, was allowed to build their clubhouse around the lighthouse. It is the most northern building set among a dozen rowing clubs known as Boathouse Row. My wife and I were in the city to help our daughter Cara and son-in-law Mike Brennan move into a new home, and we took advantage of the mild late December night. He's quite the outdoorsman, yet he'd never been on any of the previous Stars & Lights adventures. The lighthouse is less than a half-mile from their new place in the Fairmont district, and the walk to the river was all downhill. The lighthouse sits adjacent to Kelly Boulevard and across the river from Highway 76, with direct light all around. We had to give up on most of the star capture

because of all the light, not unusual while shooting within a large city. We spent an hour getting various angles and enjoyed the weather on the hike back up the hill while passing the steps of the art museum made famous in the movie *Rocky*.
Philadelphia, Pennsylvania, December 29, 2019, 12:33 a.m., 39° calm wind
Nikon D4, 14mm lens, ISO 320, f4, 3 secs
The lighthouse is part of a private club located along the Schuylkill River, but is easily viewable from the sidewalk and a neighboring park.

Page 34 left. Roundout Creek Sean and I pulled the Whaler from Rhode Island to the Hudson River on a late fall evening. There are two neighboring lighthouses located near town, Roundout Creek and Esopus Meadows. We splashed the boat at a town ramp in the creek, and motored by Roundout Creek Lighthouse on our way to first shoot Esopus. On our return, Sean dropped me off on a wooden breakwater across the channel from the lighthouse. He then took the Whaler to a spot in front of the lighthouse to light the scene. With a high tide, I felt thankful the waders kept my clothing dry while I sat on top of a piling that was submerged a few inches. It was tricky to find a spot to place the tripod, and one slip could mean disaster for the camera and lens. The current lighthouse was built in 1915 as a replacement for the previous one. It is the third lighthouse to be placed at this spot on the river.
Kingston, New York, November 28, 2016, 8:31 p.m., 38°, no wind
Nikon D4, 17-35mm lens at 35mm, ISO 1000, f2.8, 20 secs
Thanks to Lisa Cline and Kyle Haber of the Town of Kingston, New York for allowing night access to the lighthouse. It is located at the end of a Hudson River channel and is accessible only by boat.

Page 34 right. Bird Island It was at the end of the Milky Way season when we gathered a small team together to motor out to this little island and its historical lighthouse located off Marion, Massachusetts. First opened in 1819, the lighthouse went dark in the 1930s, but was relit in 1997. An extensive island renovation took place in 2018, and the town celebrated the lighthouse's 200th anniversary in 2019. It is now a bird sanctuary, and with many of the migratory birds being on the protected species list, we had to wait until most left for the season before visiting. We splashed the Whaler at the town boat ramp for the fifteen-minute ride to the island. As we approached, hundreds of birds took flight and scattered. Along with Sean and our friend Eddy, we spent about an hour shooting various angles of the lighthouse as the fading Milky Way presented itself nicely above.
Marion, Massachusetts, October 15, 2015, 8:32 p.m., 52°, 10mph wind
Nikon D4, 14mm lens, ISO 2000, f2.8, 25 secs
The island is a bird sanctuary and the lighthouse has limited seasonal access.

Page 35 left. Kennebec River Front Range Light
Page 35 right. Kennebec River Rear Range Light On a former US Coast Guard property at a bend in the Kennebec River is where these two towers form a range light. When a boat comes down the river, to stay in the channel, the captain should see only one light. Should two appear, it would indicate the ship is outside the channel. I'd driven from my home to the location, and had the entire scene as my palette. It was quite large, and I had strategically placed four lights to create the ambience. The lighthouse towers were built in 1898.
Arrowsic, Maine, February 2, 2016, 34°, no wind
Front: 9:04 p.m., Nikon D4, 14mm lens, ISO 3200, f3.2, 25 secs
Rear: 9:35 p.m., Nikon D4, 14mm lens, ISO 2000, f2.8, 25 secs
My thanks to association president Mike Kreindler for the night access to the beautiful property located along the Kennebec River.

Page 144,
Page 36 left. Turkey Point This lighthouse was built along the head of the Chesapeake Bay in 1833. For several years, we tried to gain permission to visit at night, but a prohibition blocked all visitors after sunset. Finally, an email to the Secretary of Maryland's Department of Natural Resources broke through the logjam

and allowed us park access. Given a narrow window of available dates, we decided to shoot on a late October night when the weather forecast called for clear skies. I met another lighthouse photographer who lived about an hour away at the park entrance. I'd driven six hours from home to the location, arriving just as a park ranger locked the gate to the path as we arrived. Once he made sure we were the guys with the permit, he allowed us on our way to the lighthouse. It's about a ten-minute walk on a wooded dirt road to the point overlooking the Bay. It was a crystal-clear night, and the fading remnants of the late fall Milky Way could be seen above the tower. We lit it with a dimmed LED light on a stand, and worked various angles of the property.

North East, Maryland, October 23, 2019, 8:24 p.m., 52°, no wind
Nikon D4, 14mm lens, ISO 3200, f2.8, 20 secs

My sincere appreciation to Maryland's Department of Natural Resources Secretary Jeannie Riccio and assistant Steve McCoy for allowing access to the park at night. Thanks also to Margit Pruett and Jeanette Taylor for their help from the Elk Neck State Park. Nationally recognized lighthouse photographer Pete Lerro joined me on the point for this shoot.

Page 36 right. Brant Point As the project kept growing, a trip to Nantucket, Massachusetts was in order. There are three lighthouses on the island, and we shot all on a beautiful late summer night. My buddy Sean Daly's family has a home there, and his brother-in-law Tom met us at the town's ferry landing to serve as our guide for the night. A 4x4 vehicle is a must for the island, and earlier in the evening, we loaded up provisions for a cookout before shooting Great Point Light. We also shot at Sankaty Light before making our way to Brant Point. Now early morning, Sean and I dropped off Tom, and continued our island journey to the lighthouse near the center of town. While the first two lighthouses are away from town lights, Brant is in the direct line of bright lights from a number of ships docked in the harbor. Such is the case of many of these shoots—one never knows what kind of lighting conditions will be faced until arriving at the location. The typical shot of this lighthouse includes the wooden walkway leading to the tower, but that was bathed in bright lights from the town. Getting stars would be impossible with such a bright setting, and only while shooting from the darker water side, did we achieve some better images. Despite all the town lights, we found a strong Milky Way over the circa 1901 lighthouse. It is the ninth tower at the location—the original dates back to 1746, with the previous eight having been destroyed over the years by various storms.

Nantucket, Massachusetts, Sept 16, 2015, 12:31 a.m., 68°, calm conditions
Nikon D4, 14mm lens, ISO 2000, f2.8, 30 secs

The lighthouse is on a beachfront near the entrance to Nantucket Harbor and is publicly accessible.

Page 37 left. New London Harbor Early in the project, before ever fully realizing its importance or that it was even a project, I was quickly running out of Rhode Island subjects. My sights turned to the west and Connecticut, and on a cold January night, I visited four land-based lighthouses fairly close to my home. New London, Connecticut is less than an hour away, and I'd reached out to the owners of this circa 1800 lighthouse, telling them about the project, and requesting the tower's interior lights be on for the night. Two weeks earlier, I'd spent the day surveying the property. I also received permission from the owners of the house, next to the tower, to shoot on the beach. They had been connected until 1912 when the US Coast Guard automated the lighthouse and no longer needed housing for a keeper, thus separating the two. From the beach here at Pequot Point, one can see five lighthouses on Long Island Sound. While striving to shoot most in the darkest conditions, sometimes you don't know what you'll find at night, even after seeing it during the day. The branch shadows coming from a bright streetlight on Pequot Avenue made for an interesting pattern on the tower, and I lit the foreground beach with a flashlight. Off in the distance, the bright lights from the submarine builder General Dynamics made star capture quite difficult.

New London, Connecticut, January 22, 2015, 10:04 p.m., 28°, calm wind
Nikon D4 17-35mm lens at 17, ISO 500, f2.8, 25 secs

This project owes much of its success to the willingness of this lighthouse owner's executive director, Sue Tamulevich, to offer help. From allowing us access to their lighthouses, to offering gallery space for image displays, to inviting me to speak at several lighthouse events, her support has been unwavering and is greatly appreciated. Thanks also to John and Elizabeth Ring for allowing access to their beach for the best angle of the lighthouse.

Page 37 right,
FOREWARD page 1. Buffalo Main For much of 2017, I spent many hours driving longer distances to lighthouses I never knew existed. I'd been in western New York State shooting other lights, and on a whim, I did something unusual by heading to Buffalo completely unprepared. I called the US Coast Guard Buffalo, New York office looking for information. They linked me with the president of the Buffalo Main Lighthouse, Mike Vogel, and when told of my project, he eagerly offered to help me complete it. Turns out Mike Vogel was also on the United States Lighthouse Society board, and our connection led to this larger collaboration. We both share a similar love and passion for keeping the history alive. He and his wife met me at the locked gate near the US Coast Guard compound, and we loaded up a golf cart for the trip to the lighthouse. It's surrounded by bright LED lights, and thankfully I covered them all for better photographic control. If it's too bright, star capture is all but impossible. Excessive ambient light from the city also made seeing any stars difficult, so I concentrated on capturing the tower. The lighthouse was built in 1849 and underwent an extensive renovation in 2016.
Buffalo, New York, September 17, 2017, 9:28 p.m., 70°, calm wind
Nikon D4, 14mm lens, ISO 250, f2.8, 8 secs
Many thanks to the US Coast Guard Buffalo office, and to Mike and Sandy Vogel for helping out this stranger after a late afternoon cold call to visit the lighthouse. Bill Zimmerman of Seven Seas Sailing also pointed me to the Vogels, and a big shout out to him as well.

Page 38 left. Plum Beach My lighthouse involvement all started here. In 1993, we moved our family to this town where a sad, neglected lighthouse was located. It had been abandoned over fifty years prior by the US Coast Guard, and the tower fell into total disrepair and neglect. A group petitioned the State to save it, and in 1999, received the deed to the lighthouse. I joined the group in 2001, and in 2003 watched it come to life once again through an extensive renovation. In 2004, I was asked to be its next president, a role I still hold. In 2010, we created a state license plate, sold thousands, and raised hundreds of thousands of dollars for its upkeep. Working on the lighthouse led to having many US Coast Guard contacts, and when the first *Stars & Lights* images were captured in 2013, I shared them with my new friends. This led to shooting many more lighthouses than I ever imagined, and we continue to this day. It also led to the creation of the special 20-foot tripod, initially used so we could get a night photograph of Plum Beach Lighthouse. I needed to create something to get this job done, and a local welder fashioned the aluminum tripod. It was used here at Plum Beach for the first time. The lighthouse sits in the open waters of Narragansett Bay, and although there's a nearby bridge, shooting from it is not allowed and, even if we could, the angle of the lighthouse isn't great. This image was taken the night following our successful tripod shoot of the lighthouse, as I landed at the lighthouse in darkness to obtain a different angle than what was taken from the water. I turned off the auxiliary lights on the tower, lowered the American flag, and light-painted the first level with a flashlight. The lighthouse was completed in 1899 and served for only 42 years. It was left to the elements by the US Coast Guard after the newly opened Jamestown Bridge made it obsolete in 1939.
North Kingstown, Rhode Island, June 25, 2014, 11:23 p.m., 68°, 10-15mph wind
Nikon D4, 17-35mm lens at 17, ISO 1000, f2.8, 20 secs
The lighthouse can be seen while driving over the Jamestown-Verrazzano Bridge crossing Narragansett Bay in Rhode Island. It is privately owned and closed to the public.

Page 38 right. Isle la Motte In northern Vermont on Lake Champlain sits this wonderful circa 1880 lighthouse. The Clark family owns two lighthouses in the area, and had given me permission to visit both. Earlier in the evening, I'd met owner Rob Clark at the Windmill Point Lighthouse, but here at Isle la Motte, I was on my own after Rob gave instructions on how to access the property. Despite the forecast calling for clear skies, clouds had appeared overhead as I arrived at the Point, overlooking Lake Champlain. Fortunately, they dissipated during my hour-long visit and I captured some fantastic star images.
Isle la Motte, Vermont, May 3, 2016, 11:57 p.m., 53°, calm wind
Nikon D4, 17-35mm lens at 26mm, ISO 2000, f2.8, 25 secs
Thanks to Rob Clarke for allowing access to this special lake lighthouse. It is privately owned not open to the public.

Page 39 left. Palmer Island In the middle of New Bedford, Massachusetts harbor, sits this lighthouse which opened in 1849. Access to it is pretty easy though any visit must be timed at low tide. Palmer Island is inside the massive hurricane barrier that protects the harbor during powerful storms, but at high tide, the spit between it and the mainland is covered in water. Though still accessible, it's not recommended for people to wade through it. At low tide, a cut becomes dry and easily walkable to reach the island for a short jaunt to the lighthouse. Star capture is made difficult because of high-intensity lights from the fishing docks in both New Bedford and the neighboring Fairhaven. It's rare when I don't use any of my own lights during lighthouse shoots, but the ambient light is pretty intense here, and I needed no other lights for the exposure.
New Bedford, Massachusetts, April 12, 2015, 10:20 p.m., 42°, calm wind
Nikon D4, 14mm lens, ISO 800, f2.8, 25 secs
The lighthouse is on a publicly-owned island in the middle of New Bedford, Massachusetts harbor and is accessible, though timing is based on the tide.

Page 39 right. Greens Ledge Opened in 1901, legend tells that this lighthouse, located on Long Island Sound off Norwalk, Connecticut, was named after a pirate. My first visit to try to photograph it was an important lesson in the project. Alone, I splashed the Whaler and motored out of the harbor to the light. The conditions were calm in the harbor, but once outside the breakwater, circumstances went downhill pretty quickly. Once at the light, I tried to tie off the Whaler to a ladder, but the swells nearly ripped off a cleat. I quickly shoved off, returning to the safety of the harbor. Never again would I attempt any water-based lighthouses alone. It's simply too dangerous, especially at night. A week later, and in better conditions, my brother Jack assisted on this successful shoot. He dropped me off at the ladder, and pulled away from the lighthouse to light the scene from offshore. I made my way to the end of the jetty where this pretty reflection shot was accomplished by jamming the tripod into the rocks near the water's edge.
Norwalk, Connecticut, September 25, 2016, 8:24 p.m., 59°, calm wind
Nikon D4, 14mm lens, ISO 800, f2.8, 20 secs
At the time of this shoot, the lighthouse was US Coast Guard owned. Sold in 2017, it is now owned by a private foundation and not publicly accessible.

Page 40 left,
Gallery Introduction Page 9. Big Sable While visiting Detroit, Michigan in the winter of 2018, we made plans to shoot several Great Lake lights. With US Coast Guard veteran Don App assisting, we took the drive across the state to Ludington on Lake Michigan. I'd contacted the president of the foundation caring for four lighthouses, and he was enthusiastic about the project. He met us at his town office, and we drove north along the lake to a gated state park. He unlocked the gate, and we drove two miles on a sandy path through the dunes to reach the lighthouse. It was a brisk winter night with pockets of snow still on the ground. Under my direction, Don hit the tower with a light while I donned waders and carefully walked into the frigid water. It made for a wonderful reflection with Orion in full bloom. The lighthouse was first lit in 1857, and was abandoned by the US Coast Guard in the mid 1980s as erosion imperiled the building and tower. Their plan was to let nature wreck it, but a local citizens group formed and saved it from its demise.
Ludington, Michigan, March 11, 2018, 9:09 p.m., 28°, no wind
Nikon D4, 14mm lens, ISO3200, f2.8, 20 secs
We are much appreciative of Sable Points Lighthouse Keepers Association President Pete Manting who led us out to the lighthouse on this relatively warm winter night, and who quickly learned the art of light painting with a flashlight. The lighthouse is publicly accessible, though it requires a long walk through the lakeside dunes of a state park.

Page 40 right. Burkehaven One of three lighthouses still in use as active aids to navigation on Lake Sunapee since the 1890s, the Burkehaven Lighthouse is the southernmost of the set. I'd been watching the weather closely for a number of weeks as a series of storms kept the Northeast covered in clouds most of that time. Finally, the forecast expected a clear Valentine's Night, and after getting clearance from my wife, I headed to the lake. I'd scouted the location a week earlier when in the state while covering the New Hampshire presidential primary, and parked in a small lot about a half mile from the lighthouse. It was 4° when heading out onto the ice alone, and I had an overabundance of safety gear in case I encountered thin ice. Thankfully, I did not though I heard a couple of loud cracks during

the shoot: always a disconcerting sound. I set a light on a stand to illuminate the tower and found a snow-free area of ice to lay the camera for this reflection shot.
Lake Sunapee, New Hampshire, February 14, 2020, 8:30 p.m., 0°, no wind
Nikon D4, 14mm lens, ISO 2500, f3.5, 20 secs
Thanks to June Fichter and Geoff Lizotte of the Lake Sunapee Protective Association for their tremendous assistance on all three Sunapee lighthouse shoots. More important, thanks for letting me borrow their ice claws for added safety.

Page 41 left. Rose Island One of the more popular Newport, Rhode Island tourist destinations is this 1870 lighthouse in the middle of the harbor. Run as a bed & breakfast, it's within eyesight of the Pell Bridge and can also be seen while driving to the city over Narragansett Bay. I'd talked to the foundation owners about shooting here at night, and circumstances arose when plans to visit another lighthouse fell apart. A last-minute call resulted in my quickly gathering the gear together, loading up the Whaler, hauling it to Newport, and splashing it into the harbor at a city boat ramp. It was early in this project, so I was still shooting alone on many of these adventures. I motored through the harbor to the lighthouse. It was such a spontaneous move that the president forgot to tell the nights' guests of my arrival, leaving one of the families somewhat skeptical of me. Only after showing her the results of other lighthouse shoots on my phone did she believe my tale. After darkness settled, I spent about four hours shooting various angles all around the property, and was surprised to see the Milky Way so strong despite bright lights coming from the nearby bridge.
Newport, Rhode Island, July 21, 2014, 10:21 p.m., 70°, calm wind
Nikon, 17-35mm lens at 17mm, ISO 800, f2.8, 25 secs
My thanks to Dave McCurdy, Rose Island Lighthouse President at the time of the shoot. The Lighthouse is city-owned and is publicly accessible by a seasonal ferry.

Page 41 right. Drum Point Until this point, the Stars & Lights project had never concentrated on lighthouses south of the Northeast. Sure, I'd spent time shooting a few along the Gulf Coast or in the Great Lakes, but those trips were under special circumstances. Once the project collaboration with the United States Lighthouse Society started, it was time to venture in earnest beyond the confines of the home turf. Sean and I planned a three-night trip to Delaware and Maryland with the hope of shooting up to six lighthouses. The forecast called for clear nights during an early fall spell of summer-like temperatures as the trip began. We arrived at the Calvert Maritime Museum in Solomons, Maryland where the Drum Point Lighthouse is now located as its anchor attraction. It was opened in 1883 as a working lighthouse on the Patuxent River, was decommissioned in 1978, and then moved to the museum. We arrived at the location to near 100° temperatures for the daytime survey. I noticed a dock outside of the museum's property, knocked on the door, and received permission to shoot later that night from the kind, elderly homeowner. We returned later to quiet museum grounds. They've done a wonderful job keeping alive maritime history, but for night photography, there are many direct lights with which to deal. In situations like this, you pretty much have to give up on star capture given the amount of artificial light floating around. Plus, clouds had infiltrated the area. The forecast quickly changed during our time here, and the predicted three days of clear weather fell apart. We drove the six hours home in a driving rainstorm.
Solomons, Maryland, October 3, 2019 12:16 a.m., 71°, no wind
Nikon D4, 14mm lens, ISO 1000, f2.8, 1sec
Thanks to Veronica Jordan from Drum Point Calvert Museum for giving us the late-night access to the museum and lighthouse.

Page 42 left. Boston For a number of years, the public could access Little Brewster Island where Boston Light is located, and several companies also offered island excursions. In 2018, several strong winter storms heavily damaged the docks, forcing the end of any visits. As of this writing, it still remains off-limits. Little Brewster Island is famous for having the first lighthouse established in the country in 1716. It is often listed as the oldest in the country, but because the British destroyed it during the Revolutionary War, the current tower was a rebuild opened in 1785. Sandy Hook in New Jersey remains the oldest with its original tower built in 1764. We'd gotten permission to visit Boston at night from the US Coast Guard sector command, and arrived by the Whaler on an early summer's evening. Given limited time on the island, we had to leave by 10 p.m. It was only a few days after the summer solstice, and darkness didn't allow for

good star capture until 9:45 p.m. We pre-set some lights and scrambled to capture some images once it grew dark enough. The island keeper would not allow us to continue after the allotted time, a shame because few people have attempted such imagery of the lighthouse.
Boston, Massachusetts, June 30, 2016, 9:50 p.m., 74°, 5-10mph wind
Nikon D4, 14mm lens, ISO3200 f2.8, 2 secs
Thanks to the US Coast Guard First District for making this happen: Admiral Linda Fagan, Lt. Jeannie Crump, PIO Lt. Karen Love-Kutkiewicz; US Coast Guard Auxiliary personnel Sally Snowman, Jay Thompson, and Dave Cross.

Page 42 right. Coney Island There are several lighthouses in New York Harbor, and all were designed to work together to guide ships for more than a century. Built in 1890, this lighthouse is within the perimeter of the country's oldest gated community in Brooklyn, New York. We arranged permission to visit, and at the time, it was a few years after the property had been heavily damaged by the storm surge of Hurricane Sandy. Now privately operated, the community has been trying to raise funds to repair the keeper's house, formerly a US Coast Guard station. The local police chief met us and assisted for the night, himself an amateur photographer intrigued by the project. We spent about an hour on the grounds within sight of the Verrazzano Narrows Bridge.
Brooklyn, New York, January 30, 2017, 8:41 p.m., 28°, 10-15mph wind
Nikon D4, 14mm lens, ISO 250, f2.8, 10 secs
We couldn't have completed this shoot without the great cooperation of the Sea Gate Community at Coney Island, including Joanna Crowe and Police Chief Jeff Fortunato.

Page 43 left. Doubling Point The long nights of winter are terrific for New England nighttime lighthouse photography because one can shoot several properties on the same evening. I drove north to Maine from my Rhode Island home to the town of Arrowsic where several lighthouses exist. I received permission from the private owners of the circa 1898 Doubling Point Lighthouse, and they welcomed me to their beautiful historical property. They were away for the winter and appreciated my call for the access request. It was dark and clear with millions of stars above as I went about shooting the scene. I arrived earlier to complete a daylight survey so there would be no concerning surprises in the dark. I placed an LED light on a stand on a slight hill overlooking the lighthouse, and found a pretty reflection in the water where it verged on turning to ice. The foreground grass was lit with a handheld flashlight. It was a rather mild winter when I made this visit and little snow rested on the ground. I photographed two other lighthouses this evening before heading south back home.
Arrowsic, Maine, February 2, 2016, 10:08 p.m., 31°, slight breeze
Nikon D4, 14mm lens, ISO 2000, f2.8, 25 secs
Thanks to the owners of the lighthouse, Joyce and Jim Spencer, for entrusting me to be on their property late at night.

Page 43 right. Plymouth Bug This lighthouse is often also referred as the "Duxbury Pier Light", and it has sat since 1871 near the channel, guiding boats in the large harbor for Plymouth, Marshfield, and Duxbury, Massachusetts. The narrow channel funnels swift currents by the lighthouse, and it took well over a year to plan the shoot. It had to be on or near the new moon, and we had to be in place during slack tide. That's usually a twenty-minute window when the currents have stopped while the tide switches from low to high, or from high to low. The Plymouth harbormaster had a crew lead us out of the harbor and to the lighthouse. They stayed just off frame the entire time we were shooting, fearful we might have trouble with the strong currents. We arrived as the tide was heading out, and then set the tripod in an area where we found six feet of water. As we settled the tripod legs on the bottom, we could see the strength of the water pulling at the legs. Soon, the current eased up before stopping completely. It was our time to quickly shoot: first landscape images then a tilt of the camera to shoot portrait angles. The crescent moon was about to set when we started, and it offered a beautiful reflection on the water. A few minutes after it set, the current started picking up. It had swung around and was now an inward tide. We collected the tripod and motored back to the town boat ramp where we had to wait a couple of hours until the tide was high enough to re-trailer the Whaler.

Plymouth, Massachusetts, August 9, 2016, 11:03 p.m., 70°, 5-10mph wind
20-foot tripod, Nikon D4, 14mm lens, ISO1000, f2.8, 20 secs
This shoot could not have happened without the great help of the Plymouth Harbormaster Chad Hunter and his assistants. My friend Steve Matter was my assistant on this shoot.

Page 44 left. West Quoddy As far east as you can go in the United States, Lubec, Maine, is where this lighthouse was first built in 1808, though the current tower was a replacement built in 1857. I met the president of the non-profit foundation running the property, and he gave a daylight guided tour of the grounds. He advised to be careful of porcupines just as one came waddling by. I'd never before seen one, and they pretty much keep to themselves as they are shy creatures. Throughout the evening shoot, I caught glimpses of one scampering around for food. The lighthouse beacon is a beautiful third order Fresnel lens, and shooting it at night can be problematic. Using the "dodging technique" learned many years ago in the darkroom, I used my arm to shield the camera sensor from being overexposed while burning in the stars above. Without this method, the bright beacon would blow out the exposure.
Lubec, Maine, April 18, 2017, 9:31 p.m., 38°, 10-15mph wind
Nikon D4, 14mm lens, ISO 3200, f2.8, 15 secs
Thanks to West Quoddy Head Lightkeepers Association President David Drews for the permission to be there at night, and for the porcupine avoidance tips.

Page 44 right. Bakers Island Located on an exclusive island in Salem Harbor, Massachusetts, it took several months for us to gain permission to visit at night from the foundation owners of the lighthouse. The president loved the idea of the project, but for much of the summer, the lighthouse was shrouded in scaffolding while being repainted. Finally, in late summer, with the work completed, a boat was arranged for our visit. We arrived to an army of mosquitoes, and were thankful for bug spray. It was still daylight on our arrival, and we met the full-time summer keepers. We'd pre-arranged having an evening cookout as twilight faded. Sean was with me on this shoot, and we went about setting our lights as it grew darker. The Milky Way was ending its seasonal presentation, but we captured some images of the weaker northern flank during our visit. Ambient light from Boston's North Shore also kept down our star capture. The lighthouse had recently been opened for public visitors, but only after a long court battle with neighbors of the private island where it is located. It was originally built in 1798, and for about a century had twin towers.
Salem, Massachusetts, September 17, 2015, 9:05 p.m., 74°, calm conditions
Nikon D4, 14mm lens, ISO 1000, f2.8, 25 secs
The lighthouse is owned by the Essex Heritage Commission. This shoot could not have happened without its gracious support. Many thanks to Annie Harris and Bill Steelman for their belief in this project.

Page 45 left. Pomham Rocks This lighthouse is the northernmost remaining beacon on Rhode Island's Narragansett Bay. Sitting on a small island, it was originally built in 1871, and then in 2018, underwent a major reconstruction. It is owned by the Exxon Mobil Corporation, though a non-profit maintains it. Several weeks after first having photographed it offshore using the water-tripod, we received permission to shoot on the property. We splashed the Whaler at a nearby boat ramp, and tied up to the floating dock at the lighthouse. While there's ample room to shoot three sides of the lighthouse, there's little space in the front where the most dramatic angle is located. A short fence protects visitors from coming too close to some dangerous rocks, but it almost always seems this type of spot is often the best angle for photography. We brought along an extension ladder knowing we might have to scale the fence, and it paid dividends. Bright lights of a nearby oil tank farm illuminate the area, and it was a surprise that we captured any stars. To our knowledge, this lighthouse had never before been photographed, in this way, at night.
East Providence, Rhode Island, September 22, 2014, 9 p.m., 70°, 10-15mph wind
Nikon D4, 17-35mm lens at 17mm, ISO 250, 2.8, 25 secs
My friends Keith Finck and Katherine Blythe Redlich accompanied me on this adventure, and all went well until after the shoot. As we were hauling the Whaler out of the Providence River, the conditions quickly worsened with increasing winds and waves, making for a harried end to a wonderful shoot. Many thanks to

Friends of Pomham Rocks Lighthouse President Dave Kelleher for facilitating permission from Exxon for us to be on the island at night. The lighthouse is not open to the public, but can be easily seen from the East Bay Bike Path in East Providence, RI.

Page 45 right. Monhegan As the original project continued to grow, trips to other states became more common. A buddy of mine has, for many years, rented a cottage for a week each summer on Maine's Monhegan Island. The historic 1850 lighthouse is well-documented in artwork and photographs, though nighttime images are rare. My friend, George, invited me to visit, so I grabbed a late afternoon ferry after driving to Maine from my home in Rhode Island. His week in the cottage wasn't ideal for star capture, as we had to venture out well beyond midnight after the moon set to capture our shots. The island is rather small, but also quintessential New England with primarily dirt paths, and only local homeowners have cars. We set out late for the twenty-minute walk to the lighthouse, as the stars shone brightly. When we arrived at the hill where the lighthouse is located, simultaneously clouds started filtering in overhead. Within minutes, they blocked most stars though we grabbed a few images before the skies jammed up completely. We waited about an hour, but the skies grew more ominous, so we retreated to the cabin thankful for our few images in the can.
Monhegan Island, Maine, July 13, 2016, 1:51 a.m., 70°, calm wind
Nikon D4, 17-35mm lens at 17, ISO 2500, f2.8, 20 secs
I'm indebted to my friend, George Salter, and to his friend, Larry Pierce, for inviting me out to the island in the middle of their summer vacation. The lighthouse is town-owned and easily accessible once you've reached the island by ferry.

Page 46 left. Hereford Inlet On a night when the weather forecasters called for clear skies, I arrived at this lighthouse after having earlier photographed at Absecon in Atlantic City. I'd driven five hours in brilliant sunshine only to be fogged out in the last mile of the drive. The low clouds continued, and I grew frustrated with the meteorologists. I grew up near the shore, and know that fog can happen on short notice. This issue occurred during the first book's deadline, and I had no choice but to move forward. I received permission from the foundation owners to be on the grounds after dark, and they cooperated further by dousing several bright lights. At the time of my visit, their gardens throughout the property were beautiful. Several months later, a political battle ensued and the entire foundation board was relieved of its duties. Politics aside, the lighthouse was in terrific shape during my visit, and its rotating beacon easily sliced through the gray fog. The lighthouse was first opened in 1874, and was moved to its present site 1913.
Wildwood, New Jersey, September 25, 2017, 10:08 p.m., 65°, 10-15mph wind
Nikon D4, 14mm lens, ISO 6400, F2.8, 1/6 sec
At the time of this shoot, Steve Murray was the head of the Friends of the Hereford Inlet Lighthouse, and was highly cooperative with dousing their security light the night of the shoot. The lighthouse is now run by the Town of Wildwood.

Page 46 right. Derby St. Wharf This lighthouse has guided ships in Salem Harbor, Massachusetts, since 1871. It's an easy one to photograph at any time, though bright lights throughout the harbor make star capture all but impossible. I arrived on a warm spring night after parking along a downtown street near the waterfront. The lighthouse is at the end of the town pier, and at one time, author Nathaniel Hawthorne worked as a clerk at the Custom House on this very same dock.
Salem, Massachusetts, April 21, 2015, 11:39 p.m., 62°, calm wind
Nikon D4, 14mm lens, ISO 400, f2.8, 13 secs
The lighthouse is publicly accessible on a pier in the middle of Salem.

Page 47 left,.
Page 145. Little Sable In 2018, I had the opportunity to visit Michigan a number of times when my wife worked in Detroit. I turned my attention to this state that is home to the most number of lighthouses in the United States. In late spring, a road trip led me to the eastern shores of Lake Michigan and one of its more famous lights, Little Sable. I arrived as twilight headed into darkness, and the state park was now deserted. It's always preferred to have an assistant on shoots,

but this night I was alone. It's a short hike on a boardwalk from the parking lot to the lighthouse, and the moon was growing close to its first quarter. This period isn't ideal for star capture, but it was also likely I might not ever visit this lighthouse again, so I moved forward. I carry fishing waders in the truck for the sole purpose of being able to wade into shallow water with the camera, and it's always an added bonus when I can capture a lighthouse reflection. I set a light on a stand a hundred-feet from the tower, and ventured into the water. Mindful of the danger these efforts can involve, and I wore ample safety gear, including an emergency satellite beacon in one of my pockets. I carefully made my way to a good spot for a decent camera angle of the circa 1874 lighthouse.
Mears, Michigan, June 20, 2018, 11:37 p.m., 61°, calm winds
Nikon D4, 14mm lens, ISO 2500, f2.8, 20 secs
Thanks again to Pete Manting and the Sable Points Lighthouse Keepers Association, owners of this lighthouse and three other nearby lights, for the safety tips while shooting here at Little Sable.

Page 47 right. New Canal The United States Lighthouse Society had heard of my project, and invited me to present it at its New Orleans convention in 2018. I started researching lighthouses in the area, and in doing so, reached out to several foundations. New Canal Lighthouse, established in 1838, was nearly destroyed by hurricanes Katrina and Rita in 2005. It has been completely rebuilt as part of a waterfront revitalization. For several of the nights during my visit, clouds covered the city. On my last night, they gave way to clear skies and I met the keeper at the lighthouse. To capture this image with the reflection, we first had to block rays of a nearby streetlight from ruining the shot. The keeper jerry-rigged a device at the end of a fourteen-foot pole to hold up against the light, shielding the objectionable rays. This effort created a shadow and revealed the red reflection of the beacon on the water.
New Orleans, Louisiana, February 16, 2018, 12:38 a.m., 71°, calm wind
Nikon D4, 14mm lens, ISO 200, f2.8, 4 secs
My new friends from New Orleans helped greatly during my time in the city shooting the New Canal Lighthouse. Thanks to Kate Wilson, Dwight Williams and the Lake Pontchartrain Preservation Society for believing in the project.

Page 48 left. Saugerties On New York's Hudson River, six lighthouses still lead ships along its long path. At one particularly jutted peninsula, the Saugerties Lighthouse was built in 1869, with its base made of thick granite to prevent its destruction from ice floes. I set out on a cold January afternoon from my Rhode Island home for the four-hour drive to the location. One must park at a lot near the road before following a wooded path to the lighthouse. I'd called ahead and received permission from the resident keeper to shoot into the night. I also knew lighting the building would be important for the shot and I didn't want to startle anyone. I lit the front of the lighthouse with an LED light on a stand, and crawled out on the ice to capture the reflection.
Saugerties, New York, January 5, 2016, 7:13 p.m., 12°, calm wind
Nikon D4, 17-35mm lens at 17mm, ISO 1000, f2.8, 25 secs
Thank you to keeper Patrick Landewe, his wife and young family, for allowing me access to the lighthouse on the cold winter night.

Page 48 right. Sea Girt In my first book, I unfortunately missed including several New Jersey land-based lights before deadline. Sea Girt's beacon, though no longer an active aid to navigation, has certainly retained its beauty. Nestled among large beachfront homes, the lighthouse was built in 1896. In 2012, however, much of the area was heavily damaged by hurricane Sandy. On this trip leading up to the shoot, it had been a frustrating few days of bad weather forecasts. Meteorologists had called for clear evening skies, but each night instead remained cloudy. Finally, the entire Northeast cleared and on a beautiful winter night, I set out from my home for the four-hour drive to the lighthouse. Few people were around as I went about my tasks, though I had to work to avoid light from several nearby decorative street lamps, as well as nearby bright porch lights that automatically turned on in darkness. I set a battery-powered LED light on a stand across the street from the front door.
Sea Girt, New Jersey, January 29, 2020, 7:32 p.m., 37°, 5-10mph wind
Nikon D4, 14mm lens, ISO 1000, f.5.6, 4 secs
Sea Girt is located on public street and is easily viewable.

Page 49 left. Scituate Harbor On a breakwater at the entrance to Scituate Harbor sits this historic 1827 lighthouse. It is a replacement for the original tower built in 1811. The lighthouse is town-owned and easily accessed, though the keeper's house is occupied by private tenants. Several nearby streetlights interrupt night photography, and I took this image while standing on the rocky shoreline beneath the front of the lighthouse. It came at a high cost, however, as my tripod tumbled over and smashed the lens onto the rocks just as I stepped away to light-paint the scene. Working at night in the dark and in unfamiliar grounds can be dangerous!
Scituate, Massachusetts, March 19, 2015, 10:47pm, 28°, 12-15mph wind
Nikon D4, 17-35mm at 19mm, ISO 400, f2.8, 16 secs
The Scituate Lighthouse is along a public street and is easily photographed.

Page 49 right. Old Field Village There are about twenty lighthouses on Long Island and most are still lit. In the small hamlet of Old Field Village, the town offices are located in this historic 1868 lighthouse. After receiving permission from the town manager to photograph it at night, I set out from my home on a chilly autumn evening. As I arrived, a town constable greeted me as I prepared to shoot the lighthouse sitting on the north shore of Long Island Sound. He turned off the outside lights to allow for better night images, and then I went to work. Erosion has eaten away at the front lawn, and a protective fence was built a few feet from the lighthouse front door. This limited my ability to capture images at the best angle. Because of the strong winds, I used sandbags to create stability in weighing down the tripod. The lighthouse was built with the same plans as several other area lighthouses including Great Captain Island, Sheffield Island, and Block Island North lights.
Old Field Village, New York, October 24, 2016, 10:02 p.m., 41°, 20-25mph winds, gusts to 40
Nikon D4, 14mm lens, ISO 4000, f2.8, 5 secs
The lighthouse is on Town property and is easily accessible. My thanks to Adrienne Kessel and Mayor Mike Levine for making the shoot happen.

Page 50 left. Cape Poge There are five lighthouses on Martha's Vineyard, Massachusetts. In the summer of 2014 and early in the project, I shot four during a business trip to the island. At that time, I missed capturing the Cape Poge Lighthouse as it's a bit trickier to reach. It sits on Chappaquiddick Island, quite literally a stone's throw across a water gap right next to the main island, and requires a short ferry ride to reach. I made it a point to return to the Vineyard specifically to shoot on "Chappy," as the area is locally known. I received permission from the Trustees of the Reservation, the foundation owners of many of the State's the parks, to visit the 1893 lighthouse late at night. The present tower is a replacement for the original one built in 1801. I brought my 4x4 truck to the Vineyard, another tool necessary for the drive over the barrier beach to the lighthouse on Chappaquiddick. I also brought a portable generator and electric grill, arriving at the lighthouse just before sunset. I cooked up an enjoyable dinner, finishing it as a park ranger arrived to lower the flag. He gave me a quick tour inside the tower, and we climbed to the top to relish the view. He then left to continue his other responsibilities, as I waited for twilight to fade. I shot various angles around the lighthouse, mindful of all the nearby poison ivy. Lighting the tower with a flashlight, I was pleased to capture some wonderful Milky Way images.
Chappaquiddick, Martha's Vineyard, Massachusetts, September 23, 2014, 8:05 p.m., 72°, calm wind
Nikon D4 17-35mm at 17, ISO 1600, f2.8, 20 secs
Many parks and monuments in Massachusetts are cared for by the Trustees of Reservations. The Trustees were a tremendous asset to us on this project and we're indebted to them for granting us permission to access the lighthouse for the night photography and for their assistance. The lighthouse requires a long drive over sandy dunes to access.

Page 50 right. 30 Mile Point On one of my many trips to visit my wife while she worked in Detroit, I made arrangements to spend the night at the Golden Hill State Park near Rochester, New York. One of the attractions in the park is the historic 1876 30 Mile Point Lighthouse, located 30 miles from the city. I'd recently purchased a "Roof Nest" for the top of the truck. It's basically an oversized fiberglass container that pops-up to create a hard-shelled tent containing a mattress. It takes seconds to set up, and is pretty comfortable. Once darkness fell, I set about the task of shooting the lighthouse on a rather windy night. Ironically, an astro-photographer stood nearby, though he wasn't as interested in the lighthouse as he was in the stars. I lit the tower with a stand-based LED light. Once finished, I

climbed to the top of the truck and fell asleep to the light of the blinking beacon atop the lighthouse.
Barker, New York, June 13, 2018, 11:32 p.m., 61°, 25-35mph wind, gusts to 50
Nikon D4, 14mm lens, ISO 4000, f2.8, 20 secs
My thanks to Renee Campbell, manager at the Golden Hills State Park, for granting access to the 30 Mile Point Lighthouse.

Page 51 left. Annisquam There are six lighthouses on Cape Ann in an area of Boston, Massachusetts known as the North Shore. I set out to shoot several of them on the same trip, and Annisquam was the last capture of the night. I hadn't researched the tide chart, but fortune was on my side as I arrived at dead-low tide. At high tide, water fills up around the point, offering less shore access near the lighthouse. I received permission from the Boston US Coast Guard office to be on the property and to park in the house's driveway. The lighthouse is nestled among expensive and exclusive homes in a private neighborhood. At the time of the shoot, the house was vacant, though for many years, US Coast Guard personnel occupied it. I was pleased to see the north flank of the Milky Way present in its early stages. I set an LED light on a stand behind the house to light the walkway and tower, and used a handheld flashlight to light the foreground rocks. The lighthouse was first opened in 1801, and this house is a replacement built in 1897.
Gloucester, Massachusetts, May 15, 2015, 1:57 a.m., 63°, calm wind
Nikon D4, 14mm lens, ISO 2500, f2.8, 25 secs
My thanks to the US Coast Guard First District office in Boston for night access to the lighthouse.

Page 51 right. Port Sanilac About a ninety-minute drive north of Detroit, Michigan, is this circa 1886 lighthouse on Lake Huron. My friend Don App and I took this trip after receiving permission from the private owner to be on the grounds at night. It had been a rather snowy winter at this point, and on this night, about a foot of powder was on the ground as we set lights. Port Sanilac is a small hamlet along the lake and most of the homes are summer cottages, including the lighthouse. There were several security lights ablaze on the property, and while most were within arms-reach to unscrew the bulbs, there was one that caused us to move a picnic table to climb up on to turn it off. Sometimes we just have to do what's necessary to make the shot!
Port Sanilac, Michigan, January 17, 2018, 10:40 p.m., 26°, 10-15mph wind
Nikon D4, 14mm lens ISO 800, f2.8, 20 secs
Many thanks to Port Sanilac Lighthouse owner Jeff Shook for his permission to visit on that cold January night. His insight with Michigan Lights helped to bring this book to print.

Page 52 left. Tarpaulin Cove This lighthouse is on an island in the Elizabethan Chain between New Bedford and Martha's Vineyard in Massachusetts. If you've ever been on the ferry to the Vineyard, the boat cuts between two islands, including Naushon, where the lighthouse is located. It's a private 7-mile long island, and I received permission to visit it at night. Originally, I planned to take our boat on the two-hour ride from Rhode Island to photograph the lighthouse, and I called the Woods Hole US Coast Guard to see if the lighthouse was still lit. The station chief instead offered to bring us from Woods Hole to the island while the crew was out on a nighttime drill. It was a short ride from the dock to the island, and our adventure occurred at this 1891 lighthouse on a beautiful late summer night as the US Coast Guard went about its maneuvers offshore. This tower is the second lighthouse at the location, as the present one was a replacement for the original built in 1817. The annual Perseid Meteor Showers were on full display, and we captured several shooting stars during our time at the lighthouse.
Naushon Island, Gosnold, Massachusetts, Sept. 14, 2015, 9:10 p.m., 65° light wind
Nikon D4, 14mm lens, ISO 6400, f2.8, 25 secs
Thanks to Paul Alias from the Forbes Family Trust for the late-night access to the lighthouse, and to the US Coast Guard ATON Woods Hole crew and Chief Elijah Reynolds for the ride to the lighthouse and back. We had a full camera team on this adventure, and joining me were photographers Sean Daly, Richard Kizirian, and Eddy Stahowiak.

Page 52 right. Warwick Neck This lighthouse is on a peninsula jutting out into Narragansett Bay in my home state of Rhode Island. It was my fourth lighthouse captured at night, and it was long before I realized the importance of the project. I hadn't even named the project at this point. For many years, I've been involved with a group that saved one of Rhode Island's lighthouses, and this work has created many new friendships who work in the US Coast Guard. I called the chief of the Aids to Navigation office in the State, and asked if I could have nighttime access to Warwick Neck Lighthouse. It was formerly used as US Coast Guard housing, but had been vacant for many years. The chief handed me the keys, and even called the local police to alert them of my late-night photography plans. I worked alone that night, and spent my time experimenting with "light-painting," which is basically using a flashlight to light the scene. Over the next few months, the scope of the project grew clear, as did my style of lighting the lighthouse subjects. The first lighthouse on the point was built in 1826, and the present one was a replacement built in 1932.
Warwick, Rhode Island, March 24, 2014, 10:33 p.m., 27°, calm wind
Nikon D4, 17-35mm at 17, ISO 1000, f2.8, 10 secs
My thanks to Chief Tim Chase and the Bristol, RI, US Coast Guard ATON crew for allowing access to the lighthouse. It is a US Coast Guard property and not publicly accessed.

Page 53 left. Hog Island Located on Narragansett Bay in Rhode Island, we spent this night shooting two lighthouses with the help of the custom 20-foot tripod. We had started the evening at the Conimicut Lighthouse before motoring a few miles to Hog Island. Here, it was only the third time using the tripod, and we pushed it to its limit as it's usable in water up to seventeen feet deep. We were lowering it into sixteen feet of water, plus a few inches. At Conimicut, the conditions had been rather calm, but by the time we found the shallows near Hog, the winds and seas had increased. I placed the camera atop the tripod sticking out of the water, yet waves were splashing onto the camera. This situation was certainly our most uncomfortable tripod use to date, and we quickly burst through several horizontal images before finishing with some portrait ones. The effort paid dividends as our photos likely represent the only nighttime water-based shots ever made of the historic 1901 lighthouse with the Mount Hope Bridge in the background.
Portsmouth, Rhode Island, September 17, 2014, 10:02 p.m., 60°, 10-15mph wind
20-foot tripod, Nikon D4, 17-35mm lens at 17mm, ISO 1250, f2.8, 10 secs
This shoot could not have happened without the help of my good friends Keith Finck, Eddy Stahowiak, and Hank Priest. The privately-owned lighthouse is accessible only by boat, and can be seen from shore locations in Bristol and Portsmouth, Rhode Island.

Page 53 right. Long Beach Bar Believe it or not, as I recently reviewed this image while editing other photos for this book, I noticed I'd unwittingly captured a shooting star. It is not the first time I caught something as spectacular as this background beauty without realizing it given the numerous images I take during most lighthouse shoots. We hired a boat out of Orient Point, Long Island, New York, and its captain who was quite familiar with the swift and changing currents near the lighthouse. He dropped me off on the beach while Sean stayed onboard to light the right side of the lighthouse from offshore. I placed another light on the beach about a hundred feet from the camera location to light the front of the building. The Milky Way was summer rising to vertical, and the wind blew quite strong that evening as exhibited by the stiff flag. The shooting star was definitely the big bonus. Arsonists in 1963 destroyed the original lighthouse built 1871. The present lighthouse is a 1990 rebuild. It was made an official navigation aid by the US Coast Guard in 1993.
Orient, New York, June 26, 2017, 10:23 p.m., 67°, 10-15mph wind
Nikon D4, 14mm lens, ISO2000, f2.8, 20 secs
We gained access to the lighthouse by hiring Bob Brushetta and his mate Mike Webster and their boat out of Orient Point, NY. The lighthouse can be seen from Highway 25, and is otherwise only accessible by boat. It is not open to the public.

Page 54 left. Hospital Point In a town north of Boston, Massachusetts, is this historic 1832 lighthouse that also serves as the home for the US Coast Guard's First District Admiral. I reached out to their Boston office and requested permission to shoot at night, and much to my surprise, the Admiral agreed. On my first visit, clouds overtook the point, which forced the postponement of the shoot. Instead, the Admiral offered a tour of the tower, and once we reached the top, we

chatted about all things lighthouses. She also gave me permission to visit any of the New England US Coast Guard lighthouse properties. I returned the following week under clear skies, but ambient neighborhood light kept star capture to a minimum. Also, at the edge of the grounds is a bright and direct streetlight that throws orange sodium vapor light in all directions.
Beverly, Massachusetts, May 14, 2015, 9:47 p.m., 72°, calm wind
Nikon D4, 17-35mm lens at 17mm, ISO 320, f2.8, 20 secs
My thanks to US Coast Guard Admiral Linda Fagan for allowing me onto Hospital Point to capture these rare images of the lighthouse at night.

Page 54 right. Grosse Point Prior to my wife's start of her Detroit, Michigan job, I hadn't researched many of the Great Lakes lighthouses. There are so many of them! While Michigan has, by far, the most number of historic beacons, sprinkled throughout the lakes are several in other states, including Illinois. I contacted the resident keeper at Grosse Point, told him of the project, and he quickly extended an invitation to visit. It sits next to Northwestern University in Evanston, Illinois and is slightly influenced by ambient light coming from the campus. I arrived as twilight subsided, and also requested that the security lights of the lighthouse be turned off. I spent about an hour shooting various angles of the circa 1874 lighthouse before making the five-hour drive back to Detroit.
Evanston, Illinois, April 6, 2018, 10:07 p.m., 31°, 10-15mph wind
Nikon D4, 14mm lens, ISO 500, f2.8, 13 secs
Don Terras is the keeper at Grosse Point and was instrumental in killing the lights around the property the night of the shoot. We first met at the US Lighthouse Society 2018 conference in New Orleans where he extended the invitation to shoot on the grounds.

Page 55 left. Little Gull We hired a New London captain and his boat to access both Race Rock Lighthouse in New York, as well as this nearby circa 1869 on Little Gull Island. There's been a lighthouse on the island since 1806, though the current one is a replacement. As we approached the island, what we thought were boulders on the shore suddenly came to life—they instead were hundreds of seals asleep on the beach. Once they cleared, the captain put the bow on the sand, and I jumped off with the gear. Sean stayed on the boat, and lit the island from offshore. It was late in the moon cycle, and the reflected sunlight off the moon added to the scene. The foghorn blasted every few seconds, further adding to the mystique of the shoot.
Little Gull Island, Southold, New York, April 13, 2016, 10:32 p.m., 35°, 10mph wind
Nikon D4, 14mm lens, ISO 1250, f2.8, 25 secs
Thanks to Captain Patrick Kennedy for giving us the ride to both Little Gull and Race Rock, and to Susan Tameluvich of the New London Maritime Society Museum for linking us up with his service. Thanks also to Little Gull owner Fred Plumb and David Henry for their support.

Page 55 right. Loon Island Sean and I loaded up the truck with a tool we never used before on any of these shoots—a toboggan—and left for central New Hampshire where this lighthouse, one of three on the lake, has been since 1893. The current tower is a replacement from 1960, and sits on a small island in the middle of Lake Sunapee. The foundation running the lighthouse informed us about an easily accessible place to park near the shore, and after strapping on snowshoes and loading up the sled, we trekked to the lighthouse just as the sunlight began to dip below the distant mountains. Arriving at twilight, we went to work setting lights for when the photography was to begin at darkness. Earlier the winds blew away the snow near the tower, which resulted in a wonderful reflection of the beacon on the ice.
Lake Sunapee, New Hampshire, February 20, 2017, 8:54 p.m., 26°, calm wind
Nikon D4, 14mm lens, 4000 ISO, f2.8, 25 secs
Thanks to the office of the Lake Sunapee Protective Association, especially June Fichter and Geoff Lizzotte, for their guidance in reaching the lighthouse. Located on a small island, it is viewable by boat and not open to the public.

Page 56 left. Dunkirk In the summer of 2016, I found myself in Buffalo shooting video of a Bills football game for CBS Sports. I had arrived in the city on a warm night and with clear skies. However, the moon phase wasn't ideal being close to full, but what the heck? The game's start time wasn't until later in the afternoon

the following day, so I took advantage of being close to the Dunkirk Lighthouse. I put a call into the foundation owners and received permission to shoot after sunset that night. Normally, the gates would be locked, but the grounds were hosting a Civil War reenactment and therefore open to the public for the event. Photographing here was tricky with several nearby streetlights to compensate for, as well as strong the moonlight. The lighthouse was first built on the site in 1827, but in 1875 had to be moved to its present location because of lake erosion.
Dunkirk, New York, August 19, 2016, 10:35 p.m., 78°, calm wind
Nikon D4, 14mm lens, ISO 640, f2.8, 20 secs
Association president, Dave Briska, was gracious in taking a cold call from this complete stranger before allowing late night access to the lighthouse. It is easily accessible and open to the public.

Page 56 right. Burlington Harbor North There are two channel markers that are often called lighthouses in Burlington Harbor on Lake Champlain in Vermont. I set out from home towing a trailer with an inflatable boat for easy access to the jetties where the lights are located. The red North Light is a few hundred feet from the Lake's US Coast Guard station, and along with a hired college student I'd worked with in the past, we splashed the dinghy at the town boat ramp for the short ride to the south jetty and light. We shot here first before heading to the North Light. With the lake water levels quite low from a summer drought, our climb up the large jetty rocks was a bit challenging. Winds blew from the west and waves crashed against the outer part of the jetty, but we managed to remain dry in the eastern lee. The lighthouse was first established in 1857 though it has been rebuilt several times over the years.
Burlington, Vermont, August 25, 2016, 12:44 a.m., 75°, 10-15mph wind
Nikon D4, 17-35mm lens, ISO 2000, f2.8, 20 secs
My thanks to US Coast Guard Chief Eric Barruzzi and all the support he's brought to the project over the years. Thanks to local production grip Joe Brady for his help that night on the lake.

Page 57 left. Charlotte Genesee High on a hill above the Charlotte Genesee River outside of Rochester, New York, sits this historic 1822 lighthouse. I photographed it while on a two-day trip to shoot several lighthouses. It was early morning when I arrived and I quietly went about my work mindful of the residents living in the house. There is strong ambient light from several streetlights on the property, as well as many more in the surrounding neighborhood.
Rochester, New York, September 17, 2017, 4:21 a.m., 62°, no wind
Nikon D4, 14mm lens, ISO 500, f2.8, 13 secs
Thanks to the Charlotte-Genesee Lighthouse Society for its enthusiastic cooperation allowing the nighttime shoot.

Page V.,
Page 57 right. Peck Ledge This is another lighthouse adventure involving use of my custom-built oversized tripod, and we put it through its most rigorous test to date. We splashed the Whaler in Connecticut's Norwalk Harbor for the ten-minute trip to the lighthouse. Using an electronic depth gauge, we trolled for shallow water after arriving at the circa 1906 tower, and found an area of twelve feet to its south. Sean was with me, and we deployed two anchors to stabilize the boat. We conducted a sounding measurement to confirm the depth, and set the tripod for fifteen feet as there was a rising tide. We dropped it over the side, but found the bottom to be very rocky. The tripod legs would not settle correctly, and it took about twenty attempts to finally get it to stand upright. It was an hour of tries, and in that time, the tide had risen almost a foot. I attached the camera and quickly started shooting, but the water level had risen almost a foot and the increasing swells had the boat hitting the tripod rig every few seconds. I quickly adjusted the exposure to circumvent the swells, but could only fire off eleven images before we pulled the rig back onboard. This photograph was the only portrait image taken as we had to finish fast before risking the loss of the camera and tripod. This lesson in determination left us quite happy with the results despite the cloud cover that appeared while on location. You'll also find an image of Peck Ledge in the title pages at the beginning of the book. The cloudy sky was intentionally brightened for use as a signing page.
Norwalk, Connecticut, October 4, 2016, 8:54 p.m., 62°, 10-15mph wind
20-foot tripod, Nikon D4, 14mm lens, ISO 800, f2.8, 13 secs
The lighthouse, located south of Norwalk Harbor, Connecticut, is seen primarily by boat. It is privately-owned and not open to the public.

Page 58 left. Marblehead, Massachusetts There's been a lighthouse on this point in Marblehead, Massachusetts since 1835, though through the years, its appearance has been altered. At first, it had a house and a "bird-cage" style tower, but eventually all evolved into the single skeletal 1896 tower in place today. While heading to nearby Cape Ann to shoot lights there, I swung by to survey Marblehead as the sun set. At first, I felt hesitant to shoot here, but decided that as I was on the grounds, why not? Plus, there was an unusual array of planets and stars appearing overhead, so I pulled out the camera.
Marblehead, Massachusetts, June 19, 2015, 9:38 p.m., 72°, calm wind
Nikon D4, 17-35mm lens at 35mm, ISO 100, f2.8, 8 secs
The lighthouse is in a town park and is publicly accessible.

Page 58 right. Salmon River On a trip near Lake Erie in New York State, I learned much about lighthouses I never knew existed, including this one built in 1838. It was one of several I photographed this night. I called ahead and received permission from the owners to shoot on the property near a river marina. It was early in the morning when I encountered strong and direct light from a streetlight, but combined with the air's humidity, it added a mysterious look to the scene.
Pulaski, New York, September 16, 2017, 11:30 p.m., 64°, calm wind
Nikon D4, 14mm lens, ISO 500, f2.8, 20 secs
My thanks to Abe Ellis of the Salmon River Lighthouse for allowing me to shoot at night. The lighthouse is along a public road and is easily accessible. It is run as a bed & breakfast and is available for nightly stays. They also often host open-houses for public accessibility.

Page 59 left. Montauk When shooting Montauk Lighthouse at night, the unaware person might likely walk away frustrated. At least five high-intensity security lights come on every night, which ruins any good exposures for both the lighthouse and the stars. Recognizing this reality while researching nighttime photographs of the lighthouse, I reached out to the foundation board and explained the project. They enthusiastically agreed to help, and on the day of the shoot, I met with their keeper. He gave a quick tour of the grounds, and showed me the location of the circuit panels before handing me the keys. "Put them in the flower box when you're done, and please lock the gate," he said. Once darkness fell, I went about setting up several of my lights before turning off their security ones. Suddenly, I heard a voice in the darkness. It was another photographer who'd been on the beach trying to capture a usable image of the lighthouse. Magically, the offending lights went out and the scene was beautifully lit. He ended up assisting me for the rest of the night. The first lighthouse in New York, Montauk Lighthouse was commissioned in 1792 by President George Washington and built in 1796. I dropped the keys in the flower box and locked the gate once the shoot was completed.
Montauk, New York, March 23, 2017, 10:24 p.m., 35°, 10-15mph wind
Nikon D4, 14mm lens, ISO 5000, f2.8, 25 secs
The Montauk Historical Society was terrific to work with on this project. They've even printed Christmas Cards with my images to use to raise funds. I'm so appreciative of their unlimited support, especially from Katherine Nadeau, Keeper Jason Walters, Stephanie Baloghy, Dick White, and the Montauk Lighthouse Committee. Thanks also to Bobby Alan Hamski for coming out of the dark to assist with the shoot. The lighthouse is in a state park and open to the public.

Page 59 right. Nobska Point Winter of 2015 was one of the snowiest in many years for the Northeast. After another storm, I headed out to Falmouth, Massachusetts to shoot this lighthouse located high on a hill near Woods Hole on Cape Cod. First built in 1829, the current tower was a replacement erected in 1876. For many years, the US Coast Guard used this property as housing, but it was vacant on the night of my shoot. A bright LED floodlight hit the front of both the keeper's house and lighthouse during my visit, forcing me to find a darker angle in an effort to capture the stars. I climbed a large mound of paved snow to stand above the street level for this shot.
Falmouth, Massachusetts, February 21, 2015, 12:02 a.m., 10°, calm wind
Nikon D4, 17-35mm lens at 17mm, ISO 800, f2.8, 20 secs
At the time of this shoot, the lighthouse was US Coast Guard-owned. It has since been turned over to a local non-profit, The Friends of Nobska Lighthouse, who have renovated much of the property. It is open to the public.

Page 60 left. Gurnet This lighthouse is located at the end of a peninsula facing Plymouth Harbor, Massachusetts, and sits among primarily summer vacation homes in a private neighborhood. To view it, one must have permission to visit. The foundation president allowed me the night access, and this visit was during a lull between several winter storms in 2015. Reaching the lighthouse is somewhat tricky, and involves driving over a wooden bridge before heading down a long barrier beach. The road circles a cluster of vacant cottages, making it a quiet evening for the shoot. At the end of the dirt driveway, the lighthouse sits atop one of several fifteen-foot mounds, and at one time decades ago, twin lighthouses were positioned here. The only one still remaining was built in 1842. It is said to be the oldest surviving wooden lighthouse in the country, and because of encroaching erosion, the US Coast Guard moved it to its present position in 1997. I arrived here after shooting Scituate Light in Scituate, Massachusetts, where my wide-angle lens was heavily damaged when the tripod tumbled over on the rocky shoreline. The lens zoom was stuck at 19mm, and I had to do the best I could under the circumstances.
Plymouth, Massachusetts, March 20, 2015, 12:25 a.m., 27°, 12 -15mph wind
Nikon D4, 17-35mm lens at 19mm, ISO 640 f2.8, 25 secs
Thanks to Dolly Bicknell for granting access to the neighborhood and the lighthouse. It is owned by a private foundation and occasionally holds public open house events.

Page 60 right. White River Where the White River feeds into Lake Michigan is where this lighthouse was built in 1875. It is one of four now operated by the same foundation, Sable Points Lighthouse Keepers Association, and I received permission to shoot on the grounds of all of them. Earlier in the evening, I photographed Little Sable Point Lighthouse in Mears, Michigan, before taking a short drive to White River. Its light is no longer used as an aid to navigation, and today, it is run as a museum. It was early morning by the time I finished, and a recently purchased rooftop tent-like structure enabled me to sleep on location. So, I climbed up, falling asleep in the parking lot with the light from the tower shining away.
Whitehall, Michigan, June 21, 2018, 1:40 a.m., 60°, 10-15mph wind
Nikon D4, 14mm lens, ISO 1250, f2.8, 20 secs
This is another property of the Sable Points Lighthouse Keepers Association, and thanks again to Pete Manting for assisting with the project. The lighthouse, now a local museum, is open for the public to visit.

Page 61 left. Conimicut Point Along with three friends as assistants, we motored out onto Rhode Island's Narragansett Bay to the historical 1868 tower, a replacement for one originally built in 1833. It guides ships toward Providence from a narrow peninsula between Warwick and Barrington. We arrived at low tide and deployed the custom 20-foot tripod off the side after stabilizing the boat with two anchors. It was the second time we'd ever used the tripod, and placed it into waters about eight-feet deep. A sandbar runs from the Point to the lighthouse, though the water is a few feet too deep to attempt the shot without the taller tripod. We captured some stars, but as we ventured further up the bay, and closer to several larger cities, the ambient lights became too overpowering.
Warwick, Rhode Island, September 17, 2014, 8:30 p.m., 65°, 5-10mph wind
20-foot tripod, Nikon D4, 17-35mm lens at 17, ISO 500, f2.8, 20 secs
The lighthouse is city-owned though not publicly accessible. It is viewable from a local city park or by boat.

Page 61 right. Portland Bug In the middle of Maine's Portland harbor is this circa 1875 tower, a replacement for the original built twenty years earlier. The city is an easy three-hour drive from my Rhode Island home, and I planned to shoot several lighthouses on this clear winter night. When considering shooting in Maine, people would expect really dark skies with millions of stars twinkling above at all the state's lighthouse locations. While that's primarily true, in downtown Portland, the proliferation of high-intensity lights causes the lighthouse to be bathed in light. This issue can be frustrating, but not much can be done about it. The camera picked up some stars, but with it being early in the project, it was the beginning lesson for me in dealing with a phenomenon known as "light pollution."
Portland, Maine, January 12, 2016, 2:43 a.m., 20°, 10-15mph wind
Nikon D4, 14mm lens, ISO 800, f2.8, 25 secs
The lighthouse is on public property and easily accessible along the Portland, Maine waterfront.

Page 62 left. Pemaquid Point Pemaquid is a circa 1827 lighthouse about a four-hour drive away, and I arrived on a night during the rather snowless winter of 2016. The most dramatic image of the lighthouse and tower is from the tidal pools in the rocks beneath, and it didn't disappoint. I used two lights on stands for the buildings and woods, and used a flashlight to light the foreground rocks.
Bristol, Maine, March 8, 2016, 9:59 p.m., 34°, slight breeze
Nikon D4, 14mm lens, ISO 3200, f2.8, 25 secs
The lighthouse is town-owned and publicly accessible.

Page 62 right. Fire Island On a map, Fire Island Lighthouse looked like a three-hour drive from my town. In reality, with all the traffic around metro New York, it took over five hours. We received permission from the National Parks Service through the foundation operators of the lighthouse to shoot late into the night on the property. We arrived as darkness—and cloud cover—slowly descended on the lighthouse. Ironically, it actually worked in our favor as I had to alter the exposure to be much faster than most other lighthouse shoots. That speed allowed for the capture of the beam. Had I tried for more stars, it would have required a longer exposure, and the beams would have melded into one big blob. While stars would have been nice, the way we lighted artistically overcame the star deficit over the 1826 tower. While setting the lights, a deer, only feet away, munched on some shrubs, and could not have cared less about my presence. Sean Daly was along to assist on this shoot.
Fire Island, New York, December 20, 2016, 7:14 p.m., 33°, no wind
Nikon D4, 14mm lens, ISO 2500, f2.8, 13 secs
Thanks to Dave Griese of the Fire Island Preservation Society and to John Mahoney from the National Parks Service for allowing the night access. The lighthouse is on National Parks Service land at the Fire Island National Seashore. It is open daily to the public.

Page 63 left. Stratford Point In book one, there's a terrific shot of Stratford Point Lighthouse in Stratford, Connecticut, from just outside the surrounding fence. I didn't want to repeat the image here, and had a wonderful alternative from my first visit. The US Coast Guard command staff allowed me to shoot the lighthouse at night, and at the time, the commander for the New Haven office lived in the house with his family. We met outside as I went to work, but fog rolled in almost immediately. I had to quickly recalculate the exposure to be much faster, and in several frames, the beams formed into perfect Iron Cross-like images. Because I missed any star capture, I returned on the next clear night for some spectacular stars. A lighthouse has been at Stratford Point since 1822, though the present tower was a replacement built in 1881. High seas and rough surf during Hurricane Sandy in 2012 tore away the fence and eroded the grounds surrounding the lighthouse. Most of it was repaired before my two 2015 visits.
Stratford, Connecticut, May 5, 2015, 11:59 p.m., 55°, calm wind
Nikon D4, 14mm lens, ISO 2500, f2.8, 5 secs
At the time of this shoot, the lighthouse was housing for the head of the New Haven US Coast Guard, Capt. Ed Urbanski, now retired. The lighthouse was turned over to the Town in 2019, and plans have been made to renovate much of the property to make it publicly accessible.

Page 63 right. Latimer Reef I motored a short distance to Latimer Reef just off Stonington, Connecticut from North Dumpling Island, New York, where I'd just shot the lighthouse there. Latimer Reef Light, built in 1884, is a few feet over the line into New York waters. Located in Southold, New York, with eight lighthouses, the town boasts the highest concentration of lighthouses anywhere in the United States. This adventure occurred early in the project, when I was out alone on the Whaler shooting lighthouses under very risky conditions. I later learned through experience that these types of exploits needn't and shouldn't be attempted alone. Here, at Latimer, it's tricky tying off the boat and gaining access to the ladder attached to the tower. As well, with cormorant droppings plastered all over the rocks, the ammonia smell makes for an unpleasant visit. The strong Milky Way presence worked out great, though my eyes also burned from the bird droppings, further shortening my time on the rocks.
Southold, New York, July 17, 2017, 12:39 a.m., 72°, calm wind

Nikon D4, 14mm lens, ISO 2500, f2.8, 25 secs
The lighthouse can be seen from Watch Hill, RI, Stonington, CT, and Fishers Island, NY. It is privately-owned and not publicly accessible.

Page 64 left. Plum Island Nestled among homes in the seaport town of Newburyport is this historic 1898 tower. I'd driven to the area north of Boston known as Cape Ann, where there are six lighthouses. There's much ambient and direct light to deal with while trying to shoot here at night, and I did my best to find the darkest angle of the lighthouse. The Big Dipper was in its summer orientation and I spent about an hour getting various angles before moving onto the next lighthouse.
Newburyport, Massachusetts, June 20, 2015, 12:38 a.m., 57°, no wind
Nikon D4, 14mm lens, 1000 ISO, f2.8, 20 secs
The lighthouse is run by the Town of Newburyport under a lease agreement with the US Coast Guard. Its tower is occasionally opened to the public though its grounds are readily accessible.

Page 64 right. Great Captain Island In the middle of Greenwich Harbor, Connecticut is this 1868 lighthouse, a replacement for the original one built in 1829. The Town owns the island and lighthouse, and they are cared for by a resident keeper. In warmer weather, a ferry allows residents daytime access to enjoy the beautiful island, though there is no public access at night. The keeper told us no one had ever been there after sunset, at least not during the twenty years on his watch. He met us with his 4x4 utility vehicle near the island beach, and we loaded up the gear for the drive to the lighthouse on the top of a hill. We could see Manhattan far off in the distance as we lit the building with two LED lights on stands.
Greenwich, Connecticut, September 22, 2016, 11:01 p.m., 72°, calm wind
Nikon D4, 14mm lens, ISO 640, f2.8, 20secs
My thanks for the support from Jeff Friedag with the Greenwich Parks and Recreation Department, and to keeper Mike Nickerson who was so helpful to us the night of our visit. The lighthouse is owned by the Town of Greenwich, Connecticut and is accessible by a seasonal ferry.

Page 65 left. Esopus Meadows Several lighthouses still remain on New York's Hudson River, and this one is about a hundred miles upstream from where the river meets New York Harbor. We set out towing the Whaler to a boat ramp near two lighthouses, Esopus Meadows and Rondout Creek. The former is named for the area hundreds of years ago and before the river saw its water levels increase. At one time, it was cow pastures near a river bend, and as the water rose, it became submerged. Ships started running aground, so the lighthouse was built in 1838, though the current one was a replacement opened in 1872. We found a spot with only two-feet of depth. We then stabilized the boat with two anchors and deployed the water tripod. Sean was with me on this adventure, and he jumped into the inflatable boat and rowed to a spot directly in line with the front door to illuminate the scene with a single LED light. It was one of the most tranquil shots we've ever captured while using the tripod in the water.
Port Ewen, New York, November 28, 2016, 6:58 p.m., 44°, calm wind
Nikon D4, 14mm lens, ISO 2000, f2.8, 20 secs
My thanks to the Town of Port Ewen, and to BJ Ralston for the lighthouse landing tips as well as Diane McCourt for keeping the boat ramp gate unlocked on the night of our visit. The lighthouse is cared for by a non-profit group, Save Esopus Lighthouse Commission, and it is occasionally open for public visits.

Page 65 right. Presque Isle I spent more time in 2018 visiting Detroit, Michigan and started researching Great Lake lighthouses along the drive from my home in Rhode Island. I hadn't really thought much about Pennsylvania lighthouses, but became intrigued with the idea of photographing them. I serendipitously met a lighthouse aficionado at the United States Lighthouse Society convention with contacts to Pennsylvania's Presque Isle Lighthouse. I met up with a local assistant and we arrived at the grounds located on a state park. It had been a pretty cold weather streak and about a foot of snow had accumulated on the ground, but Lake Erie's ice-pack was a little suspect. Not wanting to fall through, I found a small sandbar peninsula allowing access a few feet out onto the lake. I positioned the camera on the ice to give the illusion of being further out than it truly was. It's always a bonus when I can capture a reflection off nearby water,

even if that water is frozen at the time. The lighthouse was built in 1873 to lead ships plying the lake into the city of Erie, Pennsylvania.
Erie, Pennsylvania, March 4, 2018, 10:28 p.m., 28° 5-10mph wind
Nikon D4, 14mm lens, ISO 640, f2.8, 20 secs
My appreciation to Heather Hertel for introducing herself to me at the United States Lighthouse Society 2018 New Orleans convention, and for facilitating the connection with local expert Mike Kohler. For the first time in all of these shoots, the local police stopped us, and Mike's knowledge and "knowing the right guy" helped us out of a tricky situation. Thanks for that!

Page 66 left. Eastern Point This lighthouse is one of six lights along the shores of Cape Ann just north of Boston, Massachusetts. I arrived after shooting another nearby light, knowing there'd be no trespassing signs on the road leading to the location. I received the US Coast Guard's approval to be on the property. Now vacant, at one time, it was personnel housing. The lighthouse was first built in 1832 and the current tower is a replacement from 1890. I scaled a fence to access the property, and went to work lighting the scene. I'd recently switched to using LED lights on stands, and set one at the bottom of a slight hill. This shift allowed me to photograph various angles of the keeper's house and tower without having to reposition the light. Once I finished capturing all of the close angles, I ventured outside the fence and shot from the nearby breakwater. It was now after midnight, and earth had rotated enough to offer up a glimpse of the early season Milky Way.
Gloucester, Massachusetts, May 15, 2015, 12:03 a.m., 66°, calm wind
Nikon D4, 14mm lens, ISO 1250, 2.8, 25 secs
My thanks to the US Coast Guard First District Boston for night access to the property. It's located in an exclusive Gloucester, Massachusetts' neighborhood. It is important for visitors to ignore the "No Lighthouse Access" signs as the public road to the lighthouse leads to a nearby parking lot from which a delightful perspective of the lighthouse can be seen.

Page 66 right. Bass River My first visit to this lighthouse was in the middle of winter and the beacon was dark. Later I learned it is a seasonal light and marked on the navigation charts as being lit from May-November. I contacted the owners who allowed me onto the property to shoot. I blocked out an extremely bright spotlight, but there were far too many more to deal with, especially with guests staying at the hotel. To successfully capture the stars above while the shutter was open, I had to creatively perform a live masking with my hand over the lens to cover the hotel's bright lights. This masking process is reminiscent of the old darkroom technique known as "dodging." I was pleased to photograph the summer Big Dipper above the lighthouse which first opened in 1855 and worked seasonally since 1989.
West Dennis, Massachusetts, August 8, 2016, 10:03 p.m., 72°, 20mph wind
Nikon D4, 14mm lens, ISO 400, f2.8, 13 secs
My thanks to Greg Stone and his family for allowing me to shoot on the property in the rush of the summer season. The lighthouse is part of a seasonal hotel and is publicly accessible.

Page i.,
Page 67 left. Southeast Block Island is located about ten miles off the shores of southern Rhode Island, my home state. It's fairly easy to reach, but involves a ferry ride and car reservation. In summer, this adventure requires advance reservations. We were on a planned trip to open a gallery show of lighthouse images, and it coincided with new moon and clear skies. We arrived at the lighthouse well after dark and the Milky Way was in its great summer splendor. It was an even more special surprise to capture a shooting star near the galactic core. We were also near the height of the annual Perseid Meteor Shower. The Page 67 photograph displays an unusual angle and much of the actual lighthouse doesn't make the frame, primarily because of its position relative to the location of the Milky Way. I lit the scene with a single LED light on a stand, my tripod position was on the edge of the property, inches from a big field of poison ivy. The lighthouse was first opened in 1875, and in 1992 was moved away from an eroding cliff to its present position. The photograph at the book's beginning was taken the same night, and it demonstrates the wonderful way a Fresnel lens distributes light. The green marks on the ground are the projected rays from the lens.

Block Island, Rhode Island, August 9, 2015, 9:57 p.m., 70°, calm wind
Nikon D4, 14mm lens, ISO5000, f2.8, 25 secs
My thanks to Lisa Nolan for believing in the project and allowing the nighttime shoot. Her family lives on the property, and having a stranger appear must be disconcerting. The lighthouse is publicly accessed during daytime hours, and is one of the most notable attractions on Block Island.

Page 67 right. Tinicum Rear Range Photographing this lighthouse is both difficult and intriguing. Nestled in a clustered neighborhood between an industrial complex and the Delaware River is this 1880 tower near Philadelphia. It still functions as a range light, guiding ships plying the channel. Range lights are typically two towers working in conjunction to help ships navigate complex waterways. There are still several such lights working in the country. Tinicum is paired with a nearby Delaware River skeletal tower. With a dozen street lights surrounding the lighthouse tower, it's a significant problem for night shooting. Yet, the red beam coming from the lantern room is unlike any others we've seen, making it rather spectacular. It's difficult to see it with the naked eye, but the camera truly brought out the beam. As I approached the property, the lighthouse appeared darkened, seemingly unlit, and looked more like a water tower. The bright but narrow red beam originates from a small river-facing window at the top of the tower. At night, the black skeletal tower can look quite menacing until the contrasting redness of the light inside the lantern room appears. My daughter's husband, Mike, was along for this short adventure while I visited their Philadelphia home.
Paulsboro, New Jersey, February 22, 2020, 10:21 p.m., 34°, 5-10mph wind
Nikon D4, 14mm lens, ISO 500, f2.8, 5 secs
The lighthouse is in the middle of a recreational sports complex in the town of Paulsboro, New Jersey. It is seasonally opened for visitors.

Page 68 left. Big Bay Point The former owner of Borden Flats Lighthouse near Fall River, Massachusetts, now owns this lighthouse in Powell Township, Michigan, and runs it as a bed and breakfast. This beautiful property, high on a cliff overlooking Lake Superior, opened in 1896 as shipping increased along the Great Lakes. After a seven-hour drive from Detroit, my arrival at sunset was met with clear skies. Finishing a quick meal, I then went about my work, though it was late when it started as sunset wasn't until 9:30 p.m. I often find summer shooting more difficult because of the short nights, and prefer the longer nights of winter. Summer stars, however, are far more dramatic with the Milky Way, though the weather is also much more unstable. After the shoot, it was another chance to crawl into the Roofnest on top of the truck, with the beacon's light rays lulling me to sleep.
Powell Township, Michigan, June 20, 2018, 12:03 a.m., 61°, no wind
Nikon D4, 80-200mm lens at 120, ISO 2000, f2.8, 20 secs
On so many levels, I'm gratefully indebted to Nick Korstad for his unwavering support of this project. We've met on several occasions and fully commiserate with the "lighthouse keeper" concept. His delightful property always welcomes new guests, but they must call far in advance for reservations.

Page 68 right. Kenosha North Pier My three rules of lighting are "Control, control, control." I'd seen pictures of this lighthouse at night, and felt concerned about the spotlights on the tower. I contacted the owner, who now operates the lighthouse as an artists' cooperative, to ask if the lights could be shut off. She assured me that, because no one was scheduled to use the lighthouse until summer, the lights were off. I set out on my long drive from Detroit to Wisconsin, and arrived to see the lights still ablaze, making it impossible to control the lighting for the best photograph. Maybe someday I'll return here and have the control needed for better night photography, but after having taken the long drive, I had to settle for the images from this night. This lighthouse originally opened in 1848, though the present tower was a replacement opened in 1867.
Kenosha, Wisconsin, April 6, 2018 11:18 p.m., 28°, 15-20mph wind
Nikon D4, 14mm lens, ISO 640, f2.8, 3 secs
My thanks to Heather McGinn for helping at Kenosha North Pierhead Light. Her late husband, artist and painter John Burhani, likely would have enjoyed this project. The lighthouse, located at the end of a public pier, is easily accessible.

Page 69 left. West Chop I traveled to the island of Martha's Vineyard, Massachusetts, where there are five lighthouses, for a two-night television job for CNN. Fortunately, both were late-evening live shots, which allowed us to head out to capture most of the historic towers during our stay. Along with the satellite truck operator, we visited both the West Chop and Edgartown lighthouses on the same night. West Chop has a beautiful fourth-order Fresnel lens within the tower, and quite effective for magnifying the light, they can be problematic for good camera exposures. I knew the Milky Way was in full summer mode and wanted to capture it above the tower, but the beacon's rays were extremely strong, especially when hitting the camera lens. This lighthouse is the third lighthouse on these grounds. The original was built in 1817, followed by a replacement constructed in 1847, only to again be replaced in 1891 by the current one. The US Coast Guard granted us permission to be on the grounds, and earlier in the day, we visited to conduct a daytime survey. We also spoke to the neighbors to inform them of our plans so they would not be alarmed by our late-night arrival.
Tisbury, Martha's Vineyard, Massachusetts, July 30, 2014, 12:48 a.m., 70°, calm winds
Nikon D4, 17-35mm lens at 17, ISO 2500, f2.8, 15 secs
My thanks to the Woods Hole ATON US Coast Guard office for guidance accessing the lighthouse at night. Government owned, it is not open to the public. Thanks also to the satellite truck operator Chris Larose for accompanying me on the late-night shoot.

Page 69 right. Cumberland Head While under deadline in 2017 for the first book, I contacted the US Coast Guard office on Lake Champlain to be sure we hadn't missed any lighthouses. At one time, there'd been a dozen before the US Coast Guard removed all the beacons from their respective towers and placed them on skeletal ones. Over the years, those towers began failing, so the beacons were returned by the US Coast Guard to six of the lighthouses. My contact assured me that we'd captured all of those on the lake. The next day, however, he called apologizing for excluding Cumberland Head. It's so well-cared for that he hadn't needed to visit during his command on the lake. I connected with the owner who welcomed me onto the property with open arms, even mentioning no one had ever asked to shoot the lighthouse at night. It's at the end of a long driveway, and one needs permission to enter the private property to obtain the best shots. A lighthouse has been located on the point since 1838, though this one is a replacement built at this new location in 1868.
Plattsburgh, New York, July 31, 2017, 1:14 a.m., 68°, 5-10mph wind
Nikon D4, 14mm lens, ISO 2000, f2.8, 20 secs
The lighthouse is a privately-owned residence and is not publicly accessible. After a call from a complete stranger—me-- owners Matt and Amy Spiegel graciously allowed me onto the property for the late-night shoot. Matt even accompanied me as I went about my work, commenting that no one had ever before requested such a photograph.

Page 70 left. Navesink We almost didn't shoot this lighthouse, located in Highlands, New Jersey, because I didn't think it was still lit. Originally built as twin lighthouses, the south tower has been dark since 1952. While it's no longer used as an aid to navigation, an ornamental light shines each night in the North Tower. We were surprised to discover this as we drove to photograph the nearby Sandy Neck Lighthouse a few miles away. It became a nice addition to the collection. We spent only a few minutes on the property because we had little information about the grounds, especially at night. There's been a lighthouse here since 1828, and it's been reported to be the first United States lighthouse to have a Fresnel lens within the tower. Sean Daly accompanied me on this winter night.
Highlands, New Jersey, March 2, 2017, 9:23 p.m., 34°, 10-15mph wind
Nikon D4, 14mm lens, ISO 500, f2.8, 15 secs
The lighthouse is within state park and is publicly accessible.

Page 70 right. Aquinnah There's been a lighthouse on this Martha's Vineyard, Massachusetts point since 1799, though the current tower, built in 1856, was moved to a safer location in 2015. This image was captured on a second trip to shoot lighthouses on the island. While many of the country's original Fresnel lenses have been replaced by LED lights, the beautiful original glass structures can be photographically problematic. Most Fresnels are made of hundreds of pieces of sculptured glass, created to magnify its light source in many different directions. When standing a short distance from the tower while trying to take its night photograph, oftentimes the camera lens will get spanked pretty hard by the light. To avoid this issue, sometimes shooting from a low angle and straight up

provides the best results. Other times, the brightness of the beam becomes the shot. Here at Aquinnah, also known as Gay Head, the beams of the Fresnel lens are very bright, making it difficult for star capture. Plus, one must always keep a lookout for skunks as well as poison ivy, both thrive in great abundance here. This image was taken after having earlier visited Cape Poge on Chappaquiddick, Massachusetts.
Aquinnah, Martha's Vineyard, Massachusetts, September 23, 2014, 11:15 p.m., 68°, 10mph wind
Nikon D4, 10mm, ISO 1600, f2.8, 25 secs
The lighthouse is located within a town park and is publicly accessible.

Page 71 left. Cape May There's the research leading to the plan, then there's the reality. I'd reached out to the non-profit group running the 1823 Cape May Lighthouse in Cape May, New Jersey, for permission to shoot at night on the property. I asked if there were any lights that might affect the photography. They said there were three small solar path lights that shouldn't be a problem. My heart sank when arriving at the lighthouse as it sits inside a state park with five nearby streetlights ablaze. The fixtures weren't on the grounds, but the light spilled all over the property. I often say the best pictures happen when you have control over the lighting. Here we were, in the middle of the night, with direct light hitting the lighthouse from many angles. If only we could turn them off! It wasn't to be on this night, but we came away with some images despite the issues. The beacon rotates, and to successfully capture the magnified beams, a faster exposure is needed to freeze it in photographs. But the faster shutter speed meant fewer stars were being captured. While more stars are always a bonus, at the very least we walked away with documentation of the lighthouse working deep into the night.
Cape May, New Jersey, July 21, 2017, 1:02 a.m., 78°, calm wind
Nikon D4, 14mm lens, ISO 6400, f2.8, 1.6 secs
Thanks to the Mid-Atlantic Center for the Arts and Humanities as well as Susan Krysiak and Lorraine McKay for their assistance; and to the New Jersey Department of Environmental Protection, State Parks Service; with special thanks to Emily and Jim McLaughlin for letting me stay nearby in their lovely Cape May home.

Page 71 right. Great Point We took the five-mile drive out to Nantucket, Massachusetts's Great Point Lighthouse on a crystal clear, late summer night with the Milky Way in full display. After shooting several angles around the tower, we ended up on its south side with the camera pointed toward the north, which is the weaker view of the Milky Way. While most of the galactic core is in the southern flank, because the entire star cluster was so vibrant and strong, the north end shined spectacularly on this night. Earlier, we had a cookout with Sean's brother-in-law, Tom, who was our guide while on the island. A park ranger stopped by to watch us at work. His office had given us permission to be at the lighthouse late into the night. By all accounts, it was a fantastic evening! Originally built in 1874, the current tower was rebuilt in 1986 after a storm destroyed the lighthouse.
Nantucket, Massachusetts, September 15, 2015, 8:19 p.m., 72°, calm conditions
Nikon D4, 17-35mm lens at 17, ISO 3200, f2.8, 25 secs
I'm truly thankful to the Trustees of Reservations for believing in this project, and to Ranger Fred Pollnac for his essential help on the barrier beach. Thanks also to Tom Barada for being the evening's tour guide.

Page 72 left. Thacher Twins Here's a mea culpa: for this book, these two lighthouses are counted three times. It's part of the fuzzy math when putting a collection like this one together. These two towers, located off Rockport, Massachusetts since 1771, are the only remaining twin lighthouses in the country. They belong together in the frame, but they also have their unique characteristics and belong as separate entities as well. Hence, if you look through the totality of the collection, you'll see three for the price of two, so to speak! I arrived on the island with my daughter Amy who came along to assist. We tied up the Whaler to a mooring and rowed the inflatable dinghy ashore. It was before learning the importance of wearing ice crampons as we found it quite difficult to ascend the slick seaweed-covered boat ramp. Once on the island, we then ran into the rookery for hundreds of seagulls whose parents took offense of our arrival. For much of our time working on the shots, gulls constantly surveilled us. It was creepy!
Rockport, Massachusetts, June 26, 2016, 11:40 p.m., 70°, 5-10mph wind

Nikon D4, 14mm lens, ISO 5000, f2.8, 20 secs
My thanks to the Thacher Island Association and Paul St. Germain for allowing us on the island at night.

Page 72 right. Barcelona This lighthouse in Westfield, New York, was the very first in the nation to be lit with a gas flame. It has a deeded covenant ordering it to be perpetually lit by gas, supplied from local sources. There is no other lantern glass or magnification in the tower, just simply the gas flame. It is no longer considered an aid to navigation by the US Coast Guard, though it remains lighted. The lighthouse was built in 1829 to guide ships on Lake Erie. We were on a television shoot about an hour away so we could make time to swing by the little hamlet to capture the historic tower. My good friend Dante Bellini was along on this shoot.
Westfield, New York, August 29, 2016, 10:54 p.m., 62°, no wind
Nikon D4, 14mm lens, ISO 500, f2.8, 20 secs
The lighthouse sits close to Route 5 and is easily accessible.

Page 73 left. Goat Island This lighthouse is also known as the Newport Harbor Light. The present tower here on Goat Island in Newport, Rhode Island, was a replacement built in 1842 for the original one finished in 1823. I'd originally photographed the lighthouse early in the project, and at that time, I was new to night photography. I took few images in 2014, forcing a return visit for this book. It was a clear, new moon night, and I arrived just after an adjacent outdoor skating rink closed for the evening. It was a long walk from the parking lot to the lighthouse's location at the rear of a hotel property. The lighthouse, located on city grounds, and open to the public though the nearest parking lot is a few hundred yards away. A breeze blew gently off the water on this cold winter night. Its green beacon is constant, and nearby trees were lit with festive lights as part of the rink atmosphere. Though quite cold, I removed my jacket to cover a pathway lamp that was throwing too much light on the tower. I lit the lighthouse with a battery powered LED light on a stand.
Newport, Rhode Island, January 21, 2020, 10:50 p.m., 26°, 10-15mph wind
Nikon D4, 14mm lens, ISO 400, f4, 20 secs
The lighthouse, located on city property next to a hotel, is easily accessible, but requires a short walk from the parking lot.

Page 73 right. Orient Point This 1899 sparkplug lighthouse was the second placed here on Long Island, New York's eastern end. An earlier one was destroyed by storms. It is now privately owned, so we contacted the owner and gained permission to shoot on the lighthouse at night. We also hired a local boat captain familiar with the strong and unpredictable currents around the tower. We arrived after having shot the nearby Long Beach Bar Lighthouse just off Orient Point, New York. The captain dropped me off on the lighthouse ladder while Sean stayed on the boat and lit the scene from offshore. As the captain collected me off the lighthouse once the shoot concluded, his boat clipped the rocks a bit.
Orient Point, New York, June 27, 2017, 12:07 p.m., 67°, 10-15mph wind
Nikon D4, 14mm lens, ISO 5000, f2.8, 25 secs
Owner Randy Palumbo cordially allowed us nighttime access to the lighthouse. We hired boat captain, Bob Brushetta, to assure our safety on and off the lighthouse. It can be easily seen while riding on the Orient Point to New London Ferry.

Page 74 left. Herrick Cove This tower sits in waters on the northern flank of Lake Sunapee, New Hampshire. It is one of three similar lighthouses built by shipping companies in the late 1800s. It was first opened in 1893 and has undergone a number of renovations since then. I'd been on the lake several years earlier photographing the Loon Island Lighthouse, which at that time, was the only one lit all year long. I learned from the non-profit foundation owners that the other two now were on during the winter months and so I took the three-hour drive to the lake. It was a nerve-wracking hike while out on the ice alone, as the winter had been much milder than normal. The ice pack wasn't very thick, and the foundation personnel loaned me a pair of "eagle claws"—spikes fashioned on a line around the neck to be used to claw your way out of the water should you fall through the ice. Fortunately, that never happened though I felt more comfortable having this important tool during my time on the ice. I placed an LED light on a stand directly behind the tower and cranked up its brightness. The front of

the tower was lit with a handheld LED light from a 45° angle, giving the photograph a balance of light and shadow on the octagonal tower. As it was 0° when I finished, I felt thankful the winds had completely calmed on this beautiful winter night. The truck's heater also helped me thaw out after safely returning to land.
Lake Sunapee, New Hampshire, February 14, 2020, 9:41 p.m., 0°, no wind
Nikon D4, 14mm lens, ISO 2500, f4.5, 15 secs
My thanks to June Fichter and Geoff Lizzotte of the Lake Sunapee Protective Association, who loaned their ice claws, and for linking me to local homeowner Midge Eliassen, who allowed access to her lovely lakeside property that enabled my shorter walk on the frozen lake to the lighthouse.

Page 74 right. Ned's Point I am fortunate to live within a few hours of hundreds of lighthouses. Ned's Point Lighthouse is less than an hour away in Mattapoisett, Massachusetts. The historic tower, built in 1838, is located in a town park on grounds that remain open twenty-four hours daily. I arrived at night after another snowstorm in the winter of 2015, facing a brutally cold and windy evening. Unfortunately, a bright orange sodium-vapor light lies at the edge of the property and throws direct illumination everywhere. Situations like this create extreme frustration when arriving at an otherwise dark location. Such bright security light ruins all chances for successful night photography. While I understand the need for these lights, their presence is counterproductive to our mission. I set out to circumvent the issue, and found a low-angle frozen puddle solution to the objectionable light.
Mattapoisett, Massachusetts, February 20, 2015, 10:46 p.m., 10°, 10-mph wind
Nikon D4, 17-35mm lens at 17, ISO 4000, f2.8, 3 secs
This lighthouse, located in a town park is publicly accessible.

Page 75 left. Owl's Head Sitting high on a hill overlooking the entrance to Rockland Harbor, Maine this beacon, first built in 1825 was replaced by the current tower in 1852. It's one of Maine's more popular lighthouse tourist destinations and offers a commanding view of the Gulf of Maine from the tower. At night, it can make for a tricky shoot while trying to also capture the stars as the beacon doesn't blink. When combined with its fourth-order Fresnel lens, the beacon becomes extraordinarily bright.
Rockland, Maine, January 11, 2016, 8:22 p.m., 22°, 10-15mph wind
Nikon D4, 14mm lens, ISO 2000, f3.2, 15 secs
Thanks to Bob Trapani, president of the American Lighthouse Foundation, whose headquarters are in the keeper's house, for the help in shooting here. The lighthouse, open to the public, is operated under a license agreement with the US Coast Guard.

Page 75 right. Gloucester Breakwater On the jetty attached to the Eastern Point lighthouse sits this small beacon, Gloucester Breakwater, also known as Dog Bar Breakwater. More of a glorified channel marker than anything else, it was placed here in 1901. Though a pretty far walk out to the end of the breakwater, it was a lovely night and worth the trek.
Gloucester, Massachusetts, May 15, 2015, 12:25 a.m., 66°, calm wind
Nikon D4, 14mm lens, ISO 1250, f2.8, 25 secs
This lighthouse, located on a breakwater at the entrance to Gloucester Harbor, Gloucester, Massachusetts, is publicly accessible.

Page 76 left. Dice Head As it closed in on a new moon, on an afternoon when I had no firm plans to shoot some lighthouses, I found myself itching to shoot *something*. With no specific permission to visit any lighthouse properties, I did something highly unusual, and left home not knowing if I'd be granted access at this circa 1828 lighthouse, located in Castine, Maine. After a five-hour drive, I noticed lights on inside as I pulled into the driveway. I knocked on the door, grateful to be greeted by the family members, hands full of Christmas ornaments. I caught them as they decorated their tree. I explained my hope to shoot the lighthouse, and they, in the Christmas spirit, invited me to shoot for as long as I needed. The parents observed my process for about a half-hour, even offering me a glass of wine, which I declined knowing my long return drive home awaited me.
Castine, Maine, December 4, 2016, 6:21 p.m., 28°, calm wind

Nikon D4, 14mm lens, ISO 1000, f2.8, 20 secs
Thanks to Ted and Tracey Lameyer-- whom I interrupted on an otherwise peaceful night along the Maine coast—for being so gracious and accommodating. The town-owned property's grounds are open to the public; the lighthouse itself is not.

Page 76 right. Hudson-Athens We'd just deployed the big water tripod off the side of the Whaler when the current pulled two of the legs under the boat. It totally caught us off guard thinking there would be no strong current here, and I later kicked myself for not doing better research. When we'd shot Esopous Meadows Lighthouse further south on the Hudson a few months earlier, the river was much wider compared to here at Hudson Athens. Of course, the current was going to be stronger, it's much narrower here. So, there we were, Sean and me, struggling to bring the tripod back into the safety of the boat. We managed to get it onboard and secure, but now the only option for a decent photograph was to get onto the lighthouse. I'd already gotten permission to be on the property, but knew the shot wouldn't be as good as one from the water. Lesson learned! The lighthouse was built in 1874 using the same plans as that of Stepping Stones Lighthouse on Long Island Sound.
Hudson, New York, June 20, 2017, 11:04 p.m., 68°, slight breeze
Nikon D4, 14mm lens, ISO 4000, f2.8, 15 secs
My thanks to Tom Hoffman of the Hudson-Athens Lighthouse Preservation Society for his help in getting this image accomplished. The lighthouse society occasionally offers boat trips to the lighthouse.

Page 77 left. New London Ledge The foundation management for this lighthouse have been simply fabulous with the Stars & Lights project, and have, on several different occasions, held gallery shows of the collection in their museum. Unfortunately, the lighthouse location off the southern edge of the city, has proven to be one of the most difficult to shoot. Word is that it's haunted, but we try to not let that get in the way of our efforts. For us, using the 20-foot tripod is effective in water only up to about seventeen feet, and the bottom must be sandy for the best use. The light is called "ledge light" for a reason, and it sits not only at the edge of the drop-off, but it is also at the confluence of the river and Long Island Sound. If the current isn't running north to south or south to north from the river, it's running east to west or west to east from the Sound. Stabilizing the boat and deploying the tripod is difficult under most circumstances, and is all but impossible here. I had tried it once, alone and from the Whaler, in the summer of 2016, but failed. For this photograph, we were on a hired boat, we couldn't find any shallow water to set the tripod, and we simply pushed the camera to its extremes to get a shot, *any shot* of the lighthouse, while we were on location. The lighthouse was opened in 1909 and is owned and cared for by the New London Maritime Society Museum.
New London, Connecticut, October 31, 2016, 8:47 p.m., 45°, light wind
Nikon D4, 14mm lens, ISO 10000, f2.8, 1/8 sec
Susan Tamulevich from the New London Maritime Society and Museum has been simply terrific and hugely supportive over the years. She linked us up with Captain Patrick Kennedy for this attempt at shooting Ledge Light. The society offers boat tours to the lighthouse.

Page 77 right. Faulkner Island For months I'd been trying to secure permission from US Fish and Wildlife rangers to shoot on this island off the southern Connecticut coast. I'd been repeatedly denied for not only is it a bird sanctuary and they were fearful of protected birds getting harmed, but they were worried about our safety as some of the species can get very angry when strangers approach. We finally reached an agreement, but our visit had to happen before the springtime migration. Fortunately, the April new moon period had several days of 90° weather allowing us a rather comfortable visit. While Sean stayed offshore and lit the scene from the Whaler, I used the inflatable to row to shore. Part of the deal was to never go above the mean high tide mark, and I was able to get some nice images while staying in the parameters of the agreement. For this shot, because access to the 1802 tower was restricted to the beach, I donned waders and used a regular tripod while standing in chilly water to capture the second oldest lighthouse in the state. With no one else around, I could have easily scaled the steps for a closer image, but ethically that would have been wrong. Honor is very important to me, and the shot simply wasn't worth breaking it.
Guilford, Connecticut, April 17, 2017, 9:26 p.m., 70°, 5-10mph wind
Nikon D4, 14mm lens, ISO 1250, f2.8, 20 secs

A thank you to Rick Potvin of the US Fish and Wildlife for tips accessing the island, and to Jeff Heinrich of the Faulkner Island Brigade for his efforts in trying to get us there as well. The lighthouse sits on a federally protected bird sanctuary and is off limits to the public. It can be seen from the distant shores of Guilford, or closer by boat.

Page 78 left. Straitsmouth Island This 1896 tower was the second lighthouse on the island, replacing one that had been built in 1835. It was our third attempt at landing here, and our success is credited to the foundation president's tips on getting on and off the rocky island. Sean and I splashed the Whaler in Rockport Harbor for the short ride to the lighthouse. The keeper's house was undergoing a major renovation and there were construction materials scattered about and underfoot. That paled in comparison to the poison ivy and jagged rocks that were both everywhere. We arrived at sunset to be able to see our way around, and waited for darkness. We lit the tower with an LED light on a stand and lit the foreground with a flashlight. To the left of the tower on the horizon is the beacon from Eastern Point Lighthouse. To the right are the two lights from the twin towers on neighboring Thacher Island.
Rockport, Massachusetts, July 26, 2016, 11:03 p.m., 66°, calm wind
Nikon D4, 14mm lens, ISO 2500, f2.8, 25 secs
My thanks to the Thacher Island Association for allowing us permission to visit the lighthouse at night, and to Paul St.Germain for his secret tips on landing on the island.

Page 78 right. Tibbets Point This 1827 lighthouse has the only remaining working Fresnel lens on Lake Ontario, and while it's a beautiful piece of art, the lens can wreak havoc on night photography. With many lighthouse beacons being replaced by LED ones, when you encounter a Fresnel, you immediately see the results. They are really bright! I had set out to shoot several Lake Ontario lighthouses on this night, and arrived at Tibbetts Point as the sun was setting. The property is now used as a summer camp, and I'd gotten permission to shoot after dark.
Cape Vincent, New York, September 16, 2017, 9:09 p.m., 64°, calm wind
Nikon D4, 14mm lens, ISO 2000, f2.8, 20 secs
Thanks to John Tucker of the Tibbetts Point Lighthouse Society for the night access, as well as his tremendous assistance leading to a successful shoot.

Page 79 left. Highland This photo was captured on a wild night at Highland Lighthouse in Truro, Massachusetts. Just after another 2015 snowstorm, the winds on the Cape were gusting to more than 50mph. I just raced from my Rhode Island home to photograph the Aurora Borealis juxtaposed with the lighthouse. I'd never before seen the Northern Lights, and they were on the horizon for about twenty minutes before they disappeared. I'd heard reports they might make a far southern appearance, and fortunately, I reached Truro just in time to grab a few frames. Once I caught my breath, I spent another hour shooting various other angles of the lighthouse, including this one. At the time, the 1857 tower still had its original Fresnel lens in the lantern room, its inherent brightness making exposures to capture the stars quite a challenge. The lens has since been replaced with an LED by the US Coast Guard.
Truro, Massachusetts, March 17, 2015, 10:09 p.m., 29°, 35-50mph wind
Nikon D4 17-35mm lens at 17, ISO 4000, f2.8, 15 secs
The lighthouse grounds are open to the public on the Cape Cod National Seashore, and the lighthouse is operated by a non-profit group under license by the US Coast Guard.

Page 79 right. Chatham It was while another winter 2015 storm was pulling away when I awakened early in the morning. It was at least four hours from sunrise, the skies were clearing, it was new moon, and I was itching to shoot another lighthouse. I dressed and headed out to Cape Cod where the popular Chatham Lighthouse awaited in the darkness. The roads were clear on the drive as I headed east, and there was less snow on the ground. I arrived about an hour before the first light of dawn, and quickly went to work. I hadn't gotten permission to be on the grounds, unusual for the project, but I also hadn't at all planned on being here at this very moment. It all came about because of insomnia, but the visit paid dividends. I'd never paid much attention to the yellow front yard beacon, but it was shining brightly warning offshore boats of dangerous currents in the inlet passage. The lighthouse is the remaining tower of twin lights erected in 1808. The other tower was moved to Eastham and became the Nauset Lighthouse in 1923.

Chatham, Massachusetts, March 16, 2015, 5:33 a.m., 19°, 10mph wind
Nikon D4, 17-35mm lens at 17mm, ISO 500, f2.8, 25 secs
The lighthouse is an active US Coast Guard station and close to the public. It is on a public street and is easily seen from the road.

Page 80 left. North Dumpling Island In my role as a freelance network cameraman, I've been very fortunate, some might say even blessed, to have opportunities to meet many great people. Some were the television journalists I've worked with, others are the wonderful people I've photographed over the years. Dean Kamen is an inventor, entrepreneur, and businessman known for his life-saving medical devices as well as the Segway Personal Mover. He also owns this island south of New London, Connecticut and its circa 1847 lighthouse. I'd interviewed him a number of times over the years, and reached out to his assistant for permission to visit the island. An immediate and overwhelming affirmation came back, followed almost as quickly by a text from the island caretaker looking for more information. I launched the Whaler at a nearby marina and took a fifteen-minute ride to the island. The caretaker greeted me and directed me to the "Boathouse" cabin where I'd been invited to spend the night. Once darkness fell, I went to work getting various angles of the house and tower. The Milky Way was in full display, and for a number of images, even the north flank shined brightly. This low angle of the tower stood out as the most regal among the many captured that night.
Southold, New York, July 17, 2015, 2:15 a.m., 72°, calm wind
Nikon D4, 14mm lens, ISO 2000, f2.8, 25 secs
I'm truly thankful to Dean Kamen for allowing me to visit the island at night, and to Larry and Deb Taylor, the island keepers, for being so gracious in letting me stay overnight.

Page 147,
Page 80 right. Point Aux Barques This lighthouse is located a couple of drive hours north of Detroit on Lake Huron, and I'd reached out to the foundation president for permission to visit. It was mid-spring after a pretty harsh winter and large puddles were aplenty on the grounds. I'd flown in from our Rhode Island home and brought along a scarce amount of equipment for the shoot. Normally, and when I have my work truck, I also have an abundance of gear. On this night, it was a single camera and one light. I felt woefully underprepared as even the flashlight batteries were dead and the location is far from any normal civilization, especially at eleven o'clock at night. I made the best of what gear was with, and went about the property getting many different angles. This lighthouse is a perfect example of climate change as erosion has eaten away at the hillside cliffs protecting the 1857 tower from the lake. It was a replacement for the original one built only nine years earlier.
Port Hope, Michigan May 4, 2018 11:24 p.m., 52°, 5-10mph wind
Nikon D4, 14mm lens, ISO 6400, f2.8, 20 secs
My thanks to Bill Bonner of the Point Aux Barques Lighthouse Society for allowing the late-night visit. The lighthouse grounds are open to the public, though the tower has limited hours.

Page 81 left. Graves We contacted the owner of this historic lighthouse and got permission to visit the rocky location, sitting on the outskirts of Boston Harbor since 1905. The owner arranged our transportation, and we loaded up a boat with ten gear cases and motored out of an East Boston marina. Sean was my assistant on this adventure, and as we pulled up to the lighthouse on a beautiful summer day, we could see our work was cut out for us. All the gear, including a tent and sleeping bags, had to be carried up a ladder thirty-feet to the top of the deck. Once secured, we enjoyed the view as the sun started setting. I went about placing lights out on the adjoining rocks for the shoot as the tide was nearing its low. After we cooked dinner on the platform, darkness came and the shoot began. Wearing all my safety gear including ice crampons, I scurried out on the rocks shooting several angles of the tower. It's directly in the path of planes flying in and out of Logan, and much of my time was spent waiting for the frame to be clear. As the tide turned, many of the rocks previously high and dry were now underwater, and the last minutes of the shoot were spent grabbing gear before it was washed over. We edited images late into the night, and awakened to a bright early sunrise heightened by the sounds of barking seals beneath the platform.

Boston, Massachusetts, August 23, 2017, 9:06 p.m., 72°, 5-10mph wind
Nikon D4, 14mm lens, ISO 1600, f2.8, 20 secs
An out of the blue phone call to Graves Lighthouse owner Dave Waller brought terrific results. We're thankful to have had the opportunity to spend the night at such a unique location. Thanks to Jim Sullivan and Pat Breen from Boston Scuba for getting us safely on and off the lighthouse. The privately-owned lighthouse can be seen from the distant shores of Hull, Massachusetts.

Page 81 right. Verona Beach On both sides of New York's Oneida Lake are lighthouses, and at the time of my visit, only this one was lighted. I'd reached out to the keepers of the 1917 lighthouse on the eastern end of the lake, and told them of the plan to shoot at night. It was early in the offseason and many of the lakeside cottages were vacant, making the shoot much easier. I lit the tower with an LED light on a stand, and shot various angles on a night spent shooting several other lighthouses on nearby Lake Ontario.
Verona Beach, New York, September 17, 2017, 1:19 a.m., 67°, calm wind
Nikon D4, 14mm lens, ISO 2000, f2.8, 20 secs
Thanks to Verona Beach Lighthouse president Mary Alice Rolfe for the night access. The lighthouse grounds are open to the public.

Page 82 left. Sodus Point Museum One of two lighthouses within eyesight of each other in a small hamlet on Lake Erie, this stone building was completed in 1871 as a replacement for the 1825 original. I set out from my Rhode Island home, for the six-hour drive, on a beautiful and warm spring day to shoot later that night. The museum is on a hill overlooking the lake, but has nearby bright street lights, making night imagery a challenge. The front angle proved to be the best as the lighthouse shields the camera from the street lights, and I then illuminated the building with a single LED light on a stand.
Sodus Point, New York, April 23, 2017, 10:46 p.m., 62°, no wind
Nikon D4, 14mm lens, ISO 1600, f2.8, 20 secs
Thanks to Laurie Hayden of the Sodus Point Museum for the tips on accessing the lighthouse late at night. The lighthouse, operated by the Sodus Point Historical Society, is open to the public.

Page 82 right. Fort Point It's rare for me to set out on a nighttime lighthouse shoot without having permission to visit, especially regarding properties with known restrictions. I'd reached out to the keepers of this Maine state-owned beacon, but had to leave a voice-mail. I decided to head northeast from our Rhode Island home with the hope I'd hear back. It was a clear early winter night, there was a new moon, and I was itching to shoot. Fort Point is fairly close to Dice Head Lighthouse, where I had set out to shoot, also without permission. Along the drive, the Fort Point keeper called, clearing the way to be on the grounds. The beacon's fourth-order Fresnel lamp is constantly lit at night, problematic for trying to capture the stars as well. I lit the scene with the LED light on a stand, and lit the trees with a flashlight. The evening ended up quite successful with three lighthouses captured as Spring Point Ledge in South Portland was also part of the night's visits.
Stockton Springs, Maine, December 4, 2016, 8:56 p.m., 28°, 10-15mph wind
Nikon D4, 14mm lens, ISO 1600, f2.8, 13 secs
My thanks to Fort Point keepers Terry and Jeri Cole for their help accessing the lighthouse at night. It is located on a state park with limited visiting hours.

Page 83 left. Burlington South In the harbor of Vermont's largest city, Burlington, are two channel markers identified as lighthouses. Over the years, there have been several incarnations of them dating back to 1857. I set out to shoot them with the help of a local college student, and we launched the inflatable from a city boat ramp before motoring to the south jetty where this white flashing beacon is located. At this time, the lake water levels were relatively low due to a recent drought. It was about an eight-foot climb up granite rocks to the top of the jetty to reach the light, and my assistant stayed in the inflatable while lighting the scene with a battery LED. This pretty windy night at the light made me thankful the inflatable was well protected in the lee of the jetty from chop, kicked up by the wind.
Burlington, Vermont, August 25, 2016, 1:29 a.m., 75°, 10-15mph wind

Nikon D4, 17-35mm lens at 26mm, ISO 800, f2.8, 20 secs
Thanks to local grip Joe Brady for his assistance. The lighthouse, located on a harbor jetty, can be seen from land.

Page 83 right. Spring Point Ledge One of the more difficult times of the year to shoot lighthouses is close to Christmas as many owners place festive lights on their properties. Here in South Portland, Maine, several strings of lights had been placed on the historic 1897 sparkplug-style lighthouse, much to my dismay. I find these types of lights, while festive, are often too bright and not very photogenic for night photography. I parked in a nearby public lot, and walked the 900-foot jetty to the tower. It was a mild early December evening and I arrived after shooting several other lighthouses. I placed a battery-powered LED light on a stand about halfway along the jetty, but had to climb down among the riprap to avoid throwing a shadow. Despite an abundance of ambient light in the harbor, the camera easily picked up a fairly good number of stars.
South Portland, Maine, December 4, 2016, 11:39 p.m., 30°, 10-15mph wind
Nikon D4, 14mm lens, ISO 640, f2.8, 15 secs
The lighthouse, located on a jetty attached to a public park, is easily accessible.

Page 84 left. Sankaty With three lighthouses on Nantucket Island, Massachusetts, and with the project picking up momentum, I felt a visit was in order. One problem involved accommodations because during the summer, most expensive hotels require a two-night minimum stay. I recalled chatting with my friend, Sean, about his family having property on the island, so I reached out to him. He assisted on several earlier shoots, so he cleared the way for our visit to Nantucket. His brother-in-law, Tom, lives year-round on the island, and he picked us up from an arriving ferry. We'd earlier captured Great Point Lighthouse. also in Nantucket, before heading onto Sankaty Head, located on the grounds of a golf course. We lit the tower with a battery-powered LED light on a stand, and captured several different angles before discovering the compass rose. At night, it's hard to see it, but it made for a great foreground. I had to "Hail-Mary" the frame because it was on the ground. "Hail Mary" is the term used for eyeballing a shot without looking through the viewfinder. The ability to immediately review the image on the digital camera allowed me to adjust for a better angle, even if it was inches from the previous one. The tower, originally constructed closer to the water in 1850, boasted the first Fresnel Lens used in New England. Because of erosion, it was moved to its present location near the fifth hole of the golf course in 2007.
Nantucket, Massachusetts, September 15, 2015, 11:08 p.m., 68°, calm conditions
Nikon D4, 14mm lens, ISO 8000, f5, 25 secs
The lighthouse is owned by a trust and is open daily for visitors.

Cover,
Page 84 right. Marblehead (Ohio) I simply couldn't avoid placing this image in the book next to a similar one from Sankaty Head. While once again traveling to Detroit to visit my wife, a trip to the relatively-close Marblehead, Ohio and its historic 1821 lighthouse was in order. For the most part, I was alone on this mild spring night along Lake Erie. I decided to visit this property, a State park, unannounced. For most every shoot, I try to seek permission, though sometimes that fails. Admittedly, rarely have any police or other authorities approached me. But on this night, my luck ran out, or so I thought. While capturing various lighthouse angles, I heard a car approaching, and then moments later, it illuminated my own parked vehicle. "Uh-oh," I thought. A couple minutes later, two officers advanced toward me. "Don't tell me you came all the way from Rhode Island to shoot our lighthouse," said one. I explained the project then showed them some other lighthouse photos on my phone. Both were impressed by my dedication to lighthouses and this project. One officer, a US Coast Guard veteran, appreciated it even more because he had spent time repairing lighthouse beacons. Sometimes, fate wins out as they could have challenged my presence out there in the dark. They wished me well with the project, and continued on their way.
Marblehead, Ohio, May 7, 2018, 10:53p.m., 50°, 10-15mph wind
Nikon D4, 14mm lens, ISO 3200, f4, 15 secs
The lighthouse grounds, part of a State park, are open to the public.

Page 85 left. Marshall Point This image is one of the more famously, and beautifully photographed Maine lighthouses: Port Clyde, Maine's Marshall Point Lighthouse. It was prominently featured in the 1994 film *Forrest Gump*. I arrived here shortly after Christmas, so holiday lights still adorned the main keeper's house. It would have made for a nice foreground, but I didn't want the lights to detract from the walkway and tower. Grateful for low tide, I ventured out onto the rocks to capture a reflection shot on a relatively warm winter night. The lighthouse was built on the approaches to Clyde Harbor in 1832.
Port Clyde, Maine, January 11, 2016, 6:42 p.m., 24°, 15-20mph wind
Nikon D4, 14mm lens, ISO 500, f3.2, 20 secs
The lighthouse's grounds, open to the public, are run by the Town of St. George, Maine.

Page 85 right. Concord Point As the project evolved into USA Stars & Lights, I planned a trip to Havre de Grace, Maryland. With Sean along for the adventure, we hoped to shoot up to eight lights on a three-night trip, forecasted to be clear each night. Two nights in, the forecast changed, but we still captured this lighthouse and four others before a storm developed over the Mid-Atlantic. This lighthouse originally opened in 1827 and is now town-owned and cared for by a private foundation. It is awash in direct light from multiple units ablaze in the waterfront park, making it difficult for good night photography. Sean and I placed several LED lights at various spots to combat the effects of the park lights. This image, from farther away, offered one of the better angles. With so many lights on in the park, including stars in the photograph was impossible.
Havre de Grace, Maryland, October 2, 2019, 12:46 a.m., 70°, little wind
Nikon D4, 14mm lens, ISO 1600, f2.8, 1/3 sec
Local resident Larry Dobson was very helpful with tips on shooting the lighthouse. Located on the Town park, the grounds are open to the public.

Page viii,
Page 86 left,
Page 151 Minots Ledge In the television business, where I've spent my 40-year career, when a news outlet lands a big interview, it's called a "get." Successfully photographing this lighthouse on Boston's South Shore near the entrance to Boston Harbor, Massachusetts, was a nice *get*. It sits out in the open waters off Cohasset, Massachusetts, where the currents and swells can be unpredictable. Its terribly rocky bottom made the custom tripod useless. I started researching how to accomplish this shot by studying daytime pictures of the lighthouse and its surrounding waters. I noticed certain rocks in some—but not all—photographs, which meant they appeared only at low tide. I asked a local fisherman if he would be willing to take us out during the day for a survey. So, we went at low tide on a bright, hot summer day during the full-moon phase. And there it was: a pile of rocks about a hundred feet from the lighthouse. We returned six weeks later with the harbormaster, who brought her boat to within fifty feet of the rocks. Sean and I launched the inflatable over the side, loaded it up with gear, and I rowed alone to the rocks. Once there, I pulled the inflatable out of the water and went to work. I packed four lenses, and wore an abundance of safety gear including a wetsuit in case the shoot went awry. Sean and the harbormaster motored to a predetermined spot and lit the tower. If we had shot it without any light, it simply would have been a dark tower against the sky. I had 45 minutes on the rocks before the tide started to turn. As the water rose, I repacked and relaunched the inflatable for the row back to the safety of the boat. The right oar broke in half on the return, and I must have looked like a drunken rower before being collected onto the boat. To our knowledge, this detailed nighttime photograph of this historic 1860 tower, is the first successful capture of its kind.
Cohasset, Massachusetts, September 3, 2019, 9:13 p.m., 70°, 5-10mph wind
Nikon D4, 17-35mm lens at 35, ISO 3200, f2.8, 25 secs
The success of this photograph is owed primarily to the Cohasset Harbormaster, Lorren Gibbons, who fully supported this dangerous escapade to make the lighthouse a part of the collection. Safety was the key force driving the adventure, and it could not have happened without our initial proper risk assessment. Local fisherman John Barrett was instrumental in the daytime survey though we missed him the night of the actual shoot. And of course, having Sean Daly there to assist was key as well. Thanks to all for a fantastic image! At the back of the book are more photos from the successful shoot.

Page 86 right,
Page 143, Watch Hill This 1856 lighthouse, in Watch Hill, Rhode Island, one of the most easily accessible ones near my Rhode Island home, always needs extra care when attempting to shoot at night. Bright security lights are on most every night, making nighttime photography all but impossible. I called ahead seeking permission to shoot on the grounds and asked to have the security lights turned off. It was the height of the season for the best Milky Way images as the Galactic Core was in full display. Along with Sean assisting, we lit the tower with an LED stand light placed behind the oil house, and Sean light-painted the foreground rocks as I manned the camera. There's been some form of a lighthouse here since locals first lit fires in the early 1700s. The present stone lighthouse is a replacement for a wooden building built in 1808.
Watch Hill, Rhode Island, September 4, 2018, 10:49 p.m., 71°, 5-10mph wind
Nikon D4, 14mm lens, ISO 5000, f 2.8, 20 secs
Ann Johnson of the Watch Hill Lighthouse Keepers Association has been extremely supportive of this entire project and wonderfully responsive when we've needed to access the property. Bob Peacock is the resident keeper, and he's been as equally supportive. Thanks to the local hotel, The Ocean House, for its support sponsoring my night photographic workshop at the lighthouse.

Cover,
Page 87 left. Burnt Coat Harbor In 2010, a few years before the project began, I had a three-day television shoot on Swan's Island in Maine. It seemed appropriate to return here for the project's first lighthouse night capture in this state. I took the ferry on a rather mild winter afternoon to the island and arranged an overnight stay at a local bed and breakfast. The evening was perfectly dark and exceptionally clear for the shoot, and I was alone on the lighthouse grounds. I suspect a summertime visit would not have allowed me to hear only sounds of the waves splashing the rocks below and the trees stirring in the slight breeze. This 1872 structure had recently undergone a renovation and was slated to become an island community center.
Swan's Island, Maine, January 6, 2016, 9:18 p.m., 28°, calm wind
Nikon D4, 14mm lens, ISO 5000, f3.5, 25 secs
The Town-owned lighthouse is publicly accessible.

Introduction Page 5,
Page 87 right. Dutch Island The night lighthouse project all began here, on this small island, in Rhode Island's Narragansett Bay. It's one of my favorite spots when boating in summer. One afternoon while at anchor, I imagined shooting it at night. It took a few years to actually take the shot, but the genesis of the project started with that one thought. This image is from a second island night visit, and my buddy Eddy and his friend Brian came along to assist me. We carefully walked out on a scraggy, sharp-edged rock to the south of the lighthouse. I placed the camera down on the rock for the beacon reflection in a tidal pool while Eddy light-painted the tower with a flashlight. The lighthouse was first constructed in 1826 and the present tower is a replacement opened in 1857. The Page 5 image was one of the first captured for the Stars & Lights project in 2013.
Jamestown, Rhode Island, October 24, 2014, 9:06 p.m., 68°, calm wind
Nikon D4, 17-35mm lens at 17, ISO 640, f2.8, 25 secs
The lighthouse is part of a nature preserve on State land. Though accessible only by boat, it can be seen from land on both sides of Narragansett Bay in Jamestown, Rhode Island and North Kingstown, Rhode Island.

Introduction Page 6,
Dutch Island During the Summer of 2020, night photographers were buzzing about the NEOWISE Comet making a close approach to earth. It was just barely visible to the naked eye, but with the right sky conditions and the best cameras, it could be fairly easy to photograph. The Dutch Island Lighthouse made a nice foreground for the comet, and with my photographer friend Ross McLendon, we ventured to a Jamestown, Rhode Island park to shoot across the water for this

capture.
Jamestown, Rhode Island, July 13, 2020, 9:33 p.m., 66°, 5-10mph wind
Nikon D4, 80-200 lens at 100mm, ISO 400, f8, 4 secs

Cover,
Introduction Page 4,
Page 88 left. Tchefuncte River I had the honor of presenting Stars & Lights to the United States Lighthouse Society annual convention in New Orleans in 2018. I started researching possible subjects to shoot while in the area, and identified this historic Tchefuncte River Lighthouse in Madisonville, Louisiana, as one I might possibly capture—but I had to find a way to reach it as it is only accessible by boat. The first book, Stars & Lights: Darkest of Dark Nights, was featured in a national magazine published by BoatUS, and a few weeks before the New Orleans meeting, I received a call from a man having trouble ordering the book. Turns out, he lived around the corner from the lighthouse on Lake Pontchartrain and was willing to give me a ride to the location. We met at the town boat ramp on a rare clear night on the lake. It took a few short minutes to reach the lighthouse, and my new assistant helped by lighting the scene from where we'd tied his boat to some old dock pilings. I had shipped my waders to New Orleans so I could safely access the water for a reflection shot. This shoot occurred on my last night in the area. The next morning, I gave a talk about the project, and included a number of nighttime images of lighthouses from several of my New Orleans shoots during my visit. A lighthouse has lighted this location since 1837, though it has been destroyed and rebuilt multiple times over the course of its life. The current tower was finished in 1903.
Madisonville, Louisiana, February 15, 2018, 9:00 p.m., 68°, calm wind
Nikon D4, 14mm, ISO 2000, f2.8, 20 secs
The serendipitous book request from Dall Thomas led to the wonderful night and successful shoot on Lake Pontchartrain, and to meeting his wife, Ginger. My sincere thanks to them for indulging me on the exciting adventure. Thanks also to Wayne Wheeler, Henry Gonzalez, and Mike Vogel for the invitation to talk at the lighthouse convention, and to Trixie LeBlanc of the Lake Pontchartrain Basin Maritime Museum for believing in the project. The lighthouse can be seen at a distance from the Madisonville, Louisiana public boat ramp.

Page 88 right. Fort Pickering There are forty-three buildings identified in Massachusetts as active lighthouses, and as the project continued to grow, I reached out to many of them. One of the first captured was on Winter Island in Salem, Massachusetts, about a half-hour north of Boston. It's on a seasonal campground, and my arrival took place before it grew too crowded in the summer season. The park manager, who was grateful for my interest in the lighthouse, helped to make the shoot go smoothly. I learned the value of recent addition to my gear, a rock-climbing helmet, as one of my first steps near the shore, resulted in a slip and fall. It's one of the perils of night shooting on slick rocks near the waterline. The next day, I bought a pair of ice-crampons to enhance my safety when I walk on dark, rocky shores. Close to the lighthouse is a very bright streetlamp, though low enough for me to cover it with some well-placed equipment. I put an LED light on a stand on top of a nearby hill to illuminate the 1871 tower, and found a perfect tidal pool to cast a reflection: always an added bonus.
Salem, Massachusetts, June 19, 2015, 10:49 p.m., 67°, calm wind
Nikon D4, 14 mm lens, ISO 640, f2.8, 20 secs
My thanks to Patrick Mulligan for the night access to the campground and waterfront to shoot the lighthouse. Located on a town campground, it is publicly accessible during the day.

Page 89 left. Grindle Point I would think all Maine lighthouse locations would be wonderfully dark and perfect for star capture. The local water-taxi captain warned me about the excessive lights in and around the historic Grindle Point Lighthouse located on an island in Islesboro, Maine, near Rockport, Maine. I thought "How bad can it be?" It's bad. First, there are about six bright street lights illuminating the ferry parking lot adjacent to the lighthouse. Add to that, when the last ferry docks on the island for the night, it leaves ablaze multiple bright security lights. The lighthouse becomes awash in light, making it difficult for the best exposures. Fortunately, I arrived between tides, so the rocks on the darker water-side were still accessible. Maine coastal rocks can be extremely sharp, and

I discovered this fact the hard way. As I crawled out onto a scraggly rock, I unknowingly cut my waders. Nevertheless, I captured a number of images from the location before wading into the icy-cold autumn water for a better reflection shot. The water immediately dribbled in and down my pant leg, creating a startling moment on a rather warm mid-fall night. The lighthouse was first established on the island in 1850 though the present tower is a rebuild from 1874.
Islesboro Island, Maine, November 21, 2019, 7:06 p.m., 38°, 10-15mph wind
Nikon D4, 14mm lens, ISO 400, f2.8, 6 secs
My thanks to the Town of Islesboro for their great help with getting this shot accomplished, especially Town Manager Janet Anderson. Thanks to Jim Mitchell for coming by and watching the lighthouse being committed to history, and to Capt. Ben Smith and the Quicksilver for the ride back to the mainland. The lighthouse is next to the ferry terminal on the island and is publicly accessible.

Page 89 right. East Chop It was a delightful summer night, perfect for capturing the project's first Massachusetts lighthouse on Martha's Vineyard, Massachusetts. I was on the island for several days completing a series of late-night CNN live shots. At the end of one of those evenings, I ventured out after midnight to start shooting. On most lighthouse shoots, I'm usually alone. To my surprise, numerous people were in the park with this 1878 tower long after midnight. Behind me on a fence was a couple in a romantic embrace; to my left, several people laid on the grass, and though I could not see them, I could only hear their whispers; meanwhile, to the right of the lighthouse tower, another couple relaxed while smoking cannabis. I discovered later, while editing, that I'd captured the lighting of the joint in the photo—it's that small orange glow to the right of the lighthouse at ground level. It makes for a much more interesting story when it's included, and of the series of six pictures taken, this photo is the only one in which it appears.
Vineyard Haven, Massachusetts, July 29, 2014, 1:39 a.m., 68°, calm wind
Nikon D4, 17-35mm lens at 17, ISO 6400, f2.8, 20 secs
The lighthouse is in a publicly accessible park overlooking the Atlantic Ocean.

Page 90 left. Hendricks Head This visit was my second to the Point here in Southport, Maine and its historic 1829 lighthouse, Hendricks Head. Sixteen months earlier, I came here to shoot at night after locating the owners and receiving permission to work on their property. I arrived at sunset, and as it grew darker, I was disappointed to see the beacon light had blown out, leaving the tower darkened. I contacted the US Coast Guard and told it of the problem, and was assured it would be replaced. As the first book deadline approached, I asked and was granted permission for a repeat visit. On this night, I lit the house with one light and lit the fog bell building with another. I shot a series of beautiful Milky Way images, but soon into it, a fogbank rolled in off the water, effectively shutting down the shoot, or so I thought. As I carried the gear up from the water's edge, I stepped out of the fog that had remained over the Sheepscot River and into a clearing which revealed the house. Above was the Milky Way while the fog hugged the river. It was a truly magical moment for the project, and a mystical one for me as well.
Southport, Maine, July 16, 2017, 11:56 p.m., 62°, calm winds
Nikon D4, 14mm lens, ISO 4000, f2.8, 20 secs
My sincere appreciation to the lighthouse owners Ben and Luann Russell for allowing my visits to their beautiful property. The privately-owned lighthouse is viewable from a nearby road in Southport, Maine.

Page 90 right. Beavertail This lighthouse, another one located close to where I live in Rhode Island, is the easiest one to reach. At the south end of Jamestown, Rhode Island is Beavertail State Park with this 1754 lighthouse as one of its main attractions. I've shot here too many times to count, and it seems every visit brings on a new look and angle. Normally, I shoot only on nights near the new moon phase, but I took this image during a lunar eclipse. Though it was a full moon, as it passed through the earth's shadow, the reflecting sunlight off the moon turned to a deep orange, and the Milky Way made a strong late-season appearance. In 2020, an access road by the lighthouse was undermined by erosion and closed, creating further proof of climate change issues that endanger lighthouses.
Jamestown, Rhode Island, September 27, 2015, 11:51 p.m., 68°, calm wind

Nikon D4, 17-35 lens at 17, ISO 1600, f2.8, 25 secs
My thanks to the Beavertail Lighthouse Museum Association, especially Varoujan Karentz and Paula Samos, for allowing the up-close late-night access. The lighthouse, located on a State park is easily accessible. My daughter Amy was my assistant on this amazing night.

Page 91 left. Execution Rocks We visited this lighthouse and two others the same night on Long Island Sound, New York. Sean and I launched the Whaler in Greenwich Harbor, Connecticut and first motored close to the US Merchant Marine Academy to shoot Stepping Stones Lighthouse before heading here to Execution Rocks Lighthouse. Legend suggests this spot was named because during the Revolutionary War, the British executed prisoners by tying them to the rocks at low tide, then watching them drown as the tide rose. Our arrival to this 1849 lighthouse was met with the scattering off the rocks of about a hundred cormorants in a cacophony of sight and sound. Sean dropped me at the ladder and I made my way to a fairly good angle of the lighthouse where I could see Manhattan on the distant horizon. The place reeked of bird droppings, making it difficult to stand the stench. Also, from experience with other lighthouses, I knew the guano carries dangerous bacteria, a concern not to be readily dismissed. I quickly made several images from the one angle, and called Sean over to collect me off the Godforsaken rocks. We motored away toward Great Captain Island in Greenwich, our last lighthouse of the night. I gulped in the fresh air as the boat picked up speed.
New Rochelle, New York, September 22, 2016, 9:40 p.m., 78°, no wind
Nikon D4, 14mm lens, ISO 1000, f2.8, 13 secs
The lighthouse is privately-owned on Long Island Sound and viewable only by boat.

Page 91 right. Robbins Reef It never ceases to amaze me how many lighthouses have never before been captured at night. Here, near the heart of the communications capital of the world, it's impossible to find night images of this lighthouse located near the Statue of Liberty in New York Harbor, New York. I reached out to the Staten Island museum owners of this circa 1883 lighthouse for permission to land at night. It's a replacement tower for the original from 1839. We hired a captain familiar with the local waters, and I brought along my son Cory and his buddy Andy to assist. We landed at the lighthouse on a warm summer night. Andy stayed on the boat to light from offshore while Cory and I scampered out on the adjacent jetty for the shot. We had to crank up two lights to expose the scene to match the brightness of Brooklyn, New York, in the background.
Bayonne, New Jersey, August 16, 2017, 9:48 p.m., 82°, calm winds
Nikon D4, 14mm lens, ISO 640, f2.8, 2.5 secs
Many thanks to Erin Urban from the Noble Maritime Society on Staten Island, New York for giving us permission to visit the lighthouse. Thanks also to Capt. Gary Toske of Miller's Launch Service for providing us safety as we ventured on and off the rocks. Located near the Statue of Liberty in New York Harbor, this lighthouse can be distantly seen from the shores of Staten Island, New York.

Page 92 left. Round Island In 2018, the United States Lighthouse Society invited me to present the Stars & Lights to their national convention in New Orleans. I started researching lighthouses in the area, and found Mississippi to have two, both located only a short drive from New Orleans. I was to arrive on the night of Fat Tuesday during Mardi Gras, I knew entering the city would be a nightmare. I landed well after dark, and jumped into the rental car. I headed east, and after first shooting the lighthouse in Biloxi, Mississippi, found this one in the middle of a highway exit ramp. It's actually a complete relocation and rebuild as Hurricane Georges destroyed almost all of the tower in 1998. The original tower, built in 1833, was replaced by a new one in 1859. That one was decommissioned in 1944. After Hurricanes Katrina and Rita struck the Gulf in 2005, all that was left of the lighthouse was its round foundation base. Locals decided to raise the funds, move what was left of the foundation, and rebuild it on city land.
Pascagoula, Mississippi, February 13, 2018, 11:56 p.m., 62°no wind
Nikon D4, 14mm lens, ISO 125, f5.6, 5 secs
The lighthouse is located along Rt. 90 in Pascagoula, Mississippi, and is publicly accessible.

Page 92 right; and book title page. Patchogue Breakwater It's rare today to find a new lighthouse, but Patchogue Breakwater Lighthouse was less than a year old at the time of my visit. The small hamlet of Brookhaven, New York, on Long Island's south side faces the Atlantic Ocean, and in 2012, took a beating from Hurricane Sandy. With much of the waterfront heavily damaged, it took several years for a repair plan to develop. It then took a few more years to acquire federal funds, and in May 2019, this small lighthouse was built to replace the breakwater channel marker. I faced a problem here, as a dozen street lights shone away in the pier parking lot. I'm certain this place is really hopping in the summertime with tourists, but in January on a cold, winter night, it was quiet and deserted. In the hour spent here, I never saw another soul. The title page also has a Patchogue Lighthouse photograph. The book starts with the newest lighthouse in America, and ends with the oldest, Sandy Neck in New Jersey.
Brookhaven, New York, January 29, 2020, 10:46 p.m., 33°, light wind
Nikon D4, 14mm lens, ISO 400, f2.8, 15 secs
The lighthouse, located at the end of a town pier, is publicly accessible.

Page 93 left. Whitlocks Mill While under deadline for the first book, I hastily called lighthouse owners trying to gain access to gather more images. On the St. Croix River, in Calais in northeast Maine, is this historic 1898 lighthouse property. It's in a beautiful spot on the river. When I finally reached the location, the owners, a retired Navy admiral and his wife, graciously granted me access. However, they would leave in several days for their winter home and thus planned to lock the gate of the long access road to the lighthouse once they left. I threw all the gear together and rushed to Maine as the forecast was for a short window of clear skies during the new moon. I arrived as the sun slowly set. The couple invited me in for dinner as darkness took hold, and soon after went to work with the camera and a single LED light on a stand. There's an extreme tide of about 30-feet on the river, and it was heading toward low. For several images, I crawled over slippery seaweed-strewn rocks, being mindful of the danger of such an undertaking. I could see lights from Canada across the river, and I captured several delightful images before clouds rolled in earlier than expected. I eventually discovered this memorable juxtaposition of the fog bell and the lighthouse.
Calais, Maine, August 29, 2017, 9:50 p.m., 57°, calm wind
Nikon D4, 14mm lens, ISO 1250, f2.8, 15 secs
Retired Navy Admiral Len Picotte and his wife Sandra were overly gracious allowing access to their beautiful property, and I'm truly indebted to them. The lighthouse, located on private property, is closed to the public. It can be seen by boat while on the St. Croix River.

Page 93 right,
Page 150. Long Island This photograph was more than four years in the making, and we pulled it off with some very special US Coast Guard help. As the 2016 deadline approached for the first book, I started investigating shooting the last of the Massachusetts lighthouses yet to be captured. A bridge accessing Long Island had recently been demolished as it had become unstable after falling into disrepair. For years, the bridge connected the island to Quincy on the south side of Boston, Massachusetts. Boston's department of health ran a homeless shelter on the island, much to the consternation of Quincy's city leaders. When the bridge was razed, it once again made the island inaccessible. I began looking for whomever I needed for permission to visit at night, and grew frustrated by city and state bureaucracy. No one knew who was in charge of the island, and no one, all the way to the governor's office, could direct me. Frustrated, I went forward with the first book's publication without Long Island Lighthouse. Finally, in early 2020, I landed at the desk of the appropriate person with the ability to give the right permission, and we were on our way. Except now, the pandemic was shutting down much of the country, and the shoot was postponed for several months. Once the imminent danger eased, I now needed to find a safe way on and off the island. I made a few phone calls to several US Coast Guard contacts, and soon found a Boston unit in need of night training hours on the water. Voila, we found a ride to and from the island. Sean Daly was along on this shoot, and when we arrived at the newly seasonally-installed dock, we found the pier's upper gate locked. Adding to the adventure, we scaled the locked fence, and the US Coast Guardsmen were glad to help. Once firmly on the island, Sean and I hiked up the hill to the 1901 tower. It's an exact copy of Tarpaulin Cove Lighthouse near Martha's Vineyard, Massachusetts, and is the fourth lighthouse to be built on Long Island. A weed infested overgrown path circled around the back of the lighthouse, and as we made our way over downed trees, we followed the beacon light to its location. Several trees had fallen near the tower, and the knee-high grass was in desperate need of a cut. We carried several lights with us, and placed them far away from the tower to create shadowing of the trees onto the

lighthouse. We could hardly see the Boston skyline through the trees, and had several of them been felled, it would have made for a beautiful nighttime image. We had to accept the vision before us and recognize that it was a milestone achievement in just capturing the lighthouse in, what is indeed, a rare photograph.
Boston, Massachusetts, May 26, 2020, 9:58 pm, 70°, calm wind
Nikon D4, 14mm lens, ISO 1000, f2.8, 13 secs
This shoot likely would not have happened without the important US Coast Guard Boston ATON cooperation from Chief Jeff Nardello, BM1 Andrew Hill, and FN Nichols Desronerts. Many thanks to Tim Harrington of the Boston Health Commission for allowing us onto the island to capture this historic image.

Page 94. Race Rock There's a subtle placement with this being the last in the image section. The photographs and stories for both this book and *Stars & Lights: Darkest of Dark Nights,* are set between the races—Race Rock and Race Point. This image has been a showstopper when presented at most galleries, art fairs, or festivals. It is a rare and unique photograph, and to our knowledge, no one had ever before attempted its capture. It took over a year of planning to finally snap the camera shutter of the lighthouse located off eastern Long Island, New York. In the spring of 2015, I received permission to visit at night, but on the evening of the first attempted shoot, the Foundation director suddenly retracted her permission after learning I planned to try it alone. She expressed her concern about my lack of understanding regarding the danger of the swift currents swirling around the lighthouse. Nine months later and with assistance from a hired boat and captain, Sean and I made the trip back to the rocks off Fishers Island, New York. The lighthouse was an engineering marvel when it opened in 1879 with plans similar to the Stratford Shoal Lighthouse, further west on the Sound. While I stood on the bow fully wrapped in gear, the captain aimed the boat at the lighthouse ladder. The current had pushed us too far to the left, forcing him to retreat. On the second attempt, he aimed the bow to the right of the ladder as the current now pushed it into the rungs where I easily stepped off. He pulled away as I climbed up to the top before making my way to a good shooting location on the jetty to the right of the lighthouse. I captured various images while Sean lit the scene with a battery-powered LED light from the boat offshore. Once I completed my shots, the captain safely collected me off the lighthouse ladder.
Southold, New York, April 13, 2016, 9:12 p.m., 45°, 10mph wind
Nikon D4, 14mm lens, ISO 1000, f2.8, 25 secs
Thanks again to Sue Tamulevich of the New London Maritime Society for her caring support, and to Capt. Patrick Kennedy for ensuring my safety on and off the rocks. The privately-owned lighthouse is not publicly accessible, though the New London Maritime Society occasionally offers public trips to the lighthouse. It can otherwise be distantly seen from Groton, Connecticut.

Watch Hill, Rhode Island

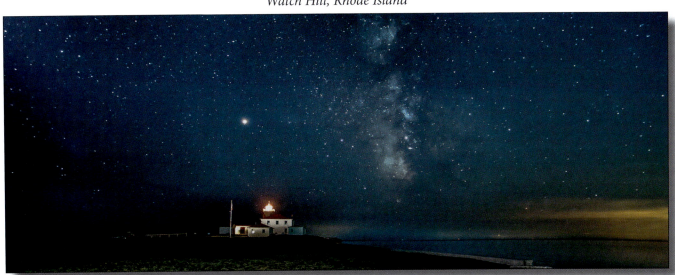

Acknowledgments

Quite possibly, the hardest part of committing all of these images into this book was keeping track of all who have helped me along the way. The seven years of researching lighthouses, gaining the permissions, planning the travel, executing the shoots, editing the images, and compiling them into *Portraits from the Dark* was a complete team effort. I'm indebted to all who helped. If, by chance, I've missed mentioning you, I offer my sincerest apologies in advance. For a majority of lighthouses, those who assisted have been previously mentioned in the stories.

For some people, it's been a long seven years: My wife Lisa has always stood by my side, and I know she's proud of what has been accomplished. Our three children are my biggest supporters, and many thanks go to Amy, Cara, and Cory, along with their significant others Joakim, Mike and Maddy.

My good friend Sean Daly has become my trusted assistant on many shoots, and our long drives and hours of conversation have been priceless. Thank you for being by my side, and thanks to his wife, Ann, for giving him up on all those long nights. Others who have assisted along the way include Keith Finck, Richard Kizirian, Eddy Stahowiak, Hank Priest, Andy Romer, George Salter, Dante Bellini, Ross McClendon, Tim Little, Steve Matter, Don App, and Joe Brady. My thanks to all the guys at Full Keel Marine in Wickford, RI, for keeping the Whaler running. Thanks to Rob Winter at Coastal Iron Works, first for creating the special 20-foot tripod, then for modifying it as we went along.

Little Sable, Mears, Michigan

When starting this in 2013, I hadn't known much about the art world, and learned quickly as the collection began to grow. It has gotten great support from many galleries, art festivals, calls for art, and regional businesses: In Rhode Island: Shayna's Place in North Kingstown; The Matunuck Oyster Bar in South Kingstown; The Cooked Goose in Westerly; the Ocean House, Watch Hill; The Hoxie Gallery, Westerly; The Providence Center for Photographic Arts; Rhode Island Home and Hospice; Scituate, Rhode Island Art Festival; Block Island Airport Gallery and the Rhode Island State Coalition for the Arts; the Wickford Art Festival; the Wickford Art Association; and Heartspace Gallery, Block Island. In Connecticut: The Connecticut Cancer Foundation and Gallery, Old Saybrook; The New London Maritime Society Museum. In Massachusetts: The Firehouse Gallery, Newburyport; Valley Photo Center, Springfield; Newton, Massachusetts Free Library; The Chatham Summer Art Festival. In New York City, the Adelante Artist Gallery. A special mention to Senator Sheldon Whitehouse for hosting a gallery of the sixteen Rhode Island lighthouse images in his Washington, DC office for more than a year. His aide Vivian Spencer chose my work for this wonderful honor.

I am truly thankful to Bay Photo of San Francisco, California. As metal prints became more popular, they were at the forefront of the latest technology, and their support has been nothing short of fabulous. Working with Matt Whittaker was a pleasure.

I desperately need to thank my attorney, Jeff Finan. His insistence that I create my first book, *Stars & Lights: Darkest of Dark Nights*, was overlooked and went unrecognized. Jeff, here is my mea culpa, and I just couldn't let it happen again. The fact that his wife, Elaine, is one of my oldest friends, makes the oversight inexcusable. I'm most appreciative of Denise Oliveira, Elaine's sister, for her expert editing and proofing. It's funny how this all works out: forty-five years ago, while I was a budding photographer, Denise was the Westerly High School yearbook editor.

This book happened because of the great and unwavering support of the United States Lighthouse Society. Since the first contact with their organization in 2017, their willingness to help with any and every aspect has been tremendous. As executive director, Jeff Gales saw the potential of *Portraits from the Dark*, and quickly agreed to get it to print. Thanks to his brother Rich, for his great design work, and to Tom Tag for starting the digitizing of all these images to be forever preserved in the Society's Candace Clifford Digital Archives. A special thanks to the USLHS board for their wonderful support as well: Mike Vogel, Henry Gonzalez, Rear Admiral William F. Merlin USCG (Ret), Ken Smith, Ralph Eshelman, Elinor DeWire, Kathy Fleming, Craig Anderson, Cheryl Shelton-Roberts, and Wayne Wheeler, President Emeritus. Much of my research is driven by the writing of Jeremy D'Entremont and his great reference book The Lighthouse New England Handbook. Many times, his lighthouse bible led me to the right neighborhood in the dark of night. Speaking of Bibles, thanks to Father Jack Unsworth for all his prayers for our safe return.

Plans had been made for dozens of shoots throughout 2020, but the Covid-19 pandemic interrupted all. Also, becoming a grandfather not only once, but twice for my daughters' daughters, Chloe and Juliet, changed so much. Their arrivals in the spring and summer of 2020 suddenly made for a refocusing of priorities. To all those hoping to have made this book, we'll get to you for the next one.

The end game of this project is far away, and right now, it feels as distant as the stars in the sky. It's come a long way since that first, wonderful night on Dutch Island. The odyssey is still just beginning, and with a little bit of luck and a lot of perseverance, someday we'll get it finished.

David Zapatka
December 2020

Index

Connecticut
Avery Point 19
Faulkner Island 77
Great Captain Island 64
Greens Ledge 39
Lynde Point 28
New London Harbor 37
New London Ledge 77
Old Saybrook Breakwater . . . 26
Peck Ledge . . . . v, 57
Southwest Ledge 18
Stratford Point 63
Stratford Shoal 24
Tongue Point 22

Delaware
Fenwick Island 29

Illinois
Grosse Point 54

Louisiana
New Canal 47
Tchefuncte River . . . Cover, 4, 88

Maine
Burnt Coat Harbor . . . Cover, 87
Cape Elizabeth 14
Dice Head 76
Doubling Point 43
Fort Point 82
Grindle Point 89
Hendricks Head 90
Kennebec River Range Front . . . 35
Kennebec River Range Rear . . . 35
Marshall Point 85
Monhegan Island 45
Nubble 27
Owls Head 75
Pemaquid Point 62
Portland Bug 61
Spring Point Ledge 83
Squirrel Point 13
West Quoddy Head 44
Whitlocks Mill 93

Maryland
Concord Point 85
Cove Point . . . . . . Cover, 14
Drum Point 41
Piney Point 19
Turkey Point 36, 144

Massachusetts
Annisquam 51
Aquinnah 70
Bakers Island 44
Bass River (West Dennis) . . . 66
Bird Island 34
Borden Flats 30
Boston 42
Brant Point 36
Cape Poge 50
Chatham 79
Cleveland Ledge 23
Derby St. Wharf 46
East Chop 89
Eastern Point 66
Edgartown Harbor 22
Fort Pickering 88
Gloucester Breakwater 75
Graves 81
Great Point 71
Gurnet 60
Highland 79
Hospital Point 54
Long Island 93, 150
Long Point 21
Marblehead 58
Minots Ledge . . . . viii, 86, 151
Nauset 24
Ned's Point 74
Nobska Point 59
Palmer Island 39
Plum Island 64
Plymouth Bug 43
Race Point 10
Sandy Neck 16
Sankaty Head 84
Scituate Harbor 49
Straitsmouth Island 78
Tarpaulin Cove 52
Ten Pound Harbor 28
Thacher Island North 11
Thacher Island South 26
Thacher Island Twins 72
West Chop 69
Wood End 21

148

Michigan

Big Bay Point	68
Big Sable	9, 40
Fort Gratiot	15
Little Sable	47, 145
Livingstone Memorial	33
Ludington North Breakwater	vi, 25
Point Aux Barques	80, 147
Port Sanilac	51
White River	60

Mississippi

Biloxi	17
Round Island	92

New Hampshire

Burkehaven	40
Herrick Cove	74
Loon Island	55
Portsmouth Harbor	27

New Jersey

Absecon	23
Barnegat	15
Cape May	71
East Point	16
Hereford Inlet	46
Navesink	70
Robbins Reef	91
Romer Shoal	32
Sandy Hook	13, 152
Sea Girt	48
Tinicum	67

New York

Barcelona	72
Bluff Point	29
Buffalo Main	1, 37
Charlotte Genesee	57
Coney Island	42
Cumberland Head	69
Dunkirk	56
Eatons Neck	11
Esopus Meadows	65
Execution Rocks	91
Fire Island	62
Horton Point	20
Hudson-Athens	76
Huntington Harbor	17
Latimer Reef	63
Little Gull	55
Long Beach Bar	53
Montauk	59
North Dumpling Island	80
Old Field Village	49
Orient Point	73
Patchogue	ii, 92
Race Rock	94
Rondout Creek	34
Salmon River	58
Saugerties	48
Sleepy Hollow	12
Sodus Bay	25
Sodus Point Museum	82
Stepping Stones	30
Thirty Mile Point	50
Tibbetts Point	78
Verona Beach	81

Ohio

Marblehead	Cover, 84

Pennsylvania

Erie North Pier	31
Presque Isle	65
Turtle Rock	33

Rhode Island

Beavertail	90
Castle Hill	3, 20
Conimicut	61
Dutch Island	5, 6, 87
Goat Island	73
Hog Island	53
North	Cover, 10
Plum Beach	38
Point Judith	18
Pomham Rocks	45
Rose Island	41
Sakonnet	32
Sandy Point	31
Southeast	i, 67
Warwick Neck	52
Watch Hill	86, 143

Vermont

Burlington Harbor North	56
Burlington Harbor South	83
Isle la Motte	38
Windmill Point	12

Wisconsin

Kenosha North Pier	68

Photographers Sean Daly and David Zapatka socially distancing at Long Island Lighthouse, Boston, May 2020

If you didn't have the chance to read about the Minots Ledge adventure on page 137, please indulge me here. This shoot was more than three years in planning, and I'm most certain when I walked into Cohasset, Massachusetts, harbormaster Lorren Gibbons' office that hot July 2019 day, she was ready to have me committed. Fortunately, I offered her a copy of *Darkest of Dark Nights* to convince her otherwise. Minots Ledge Lighthouse sits outside the harbor in rocky and treacherous waters also accompanied by a great influence of currents, not to mention constantly changing winds and seas. There's a reason why the lighthouse was placed where it sits, and countless shipwrecks over the centuries can attest to the dangers in the area. Now, here I was, a complete stranger asking her if she thought it possible to capture the shot. A quick and engaging smile brought the answer. Earlier in the day, we met local fisherman, John Barrett, at the dock and I explained our shoot intent. Seeming

intrigued, he was kind enough to bring my buddy Sean Daly and me out on a daytime survey, on a hot day in mid-July. We were trolling the water near the lighthouse during a full moon, and I told him that in two weeks, during the new moon at low tide, we needed to be at the very rocks

we were looking at near the lighthouse. Those rocks only appear at the lowest of low tides, and occur only at the extremes of full and new moons. Two weeks later, during the new moon and with a flotilla of three boats, we made our way to the lighthouse only to find sea swells--waves--crashing over the rock and we were shut out. A month later, during the next new moon and with only Lorren guiding us, we landed on the rock with better sea conditions. And yes, I'm a complete geek with the safety gear, though this was the only time I wore a wetsuit on any shoot. But, as I always say—when one reaches the Everest summit, the other half still waits! Minots Ledge was one for the history books!